CHRISTOPHER NOLAN

PHILOSOPHICAL FILMMAKERS

Series editor: Costica Bradatan is a Professor of Humanities at Texas Tech University, USA, and an Honorary Research Professor of Philosophy at the University of Queensland, Australia. He is the author of *Dying for Ideas: The Dangerous Lives of the Philosophers* (Bloomsbury, 2015), among other books.

Films can ask big questions about human existence: what it means to be alive, to be afraid, to be moral, to be loved. The *Philosophical Filmmakers* series examines the work of influential directors, through the writing of thinkers wanting to grapple with the rocky territory where film and philosophy touch borders.

Each book involves a philosopher engaging with an individual filmmaker's work, revealing how it has inspired the author's own philosophical perspectives and how critical engagement with those films can expand our intellectual horizons.

Other titles in the series:
Eric Rohmer, Vittorio Hösle
Werner Herzog, Richard Eldridge
Terrence Malick, Robert Sinnerbrink
Kenneth Lonergan, Todd May
Shyam Benegal, Samir Chopra
Douglas Sirk, Robert B. Pippin
Lucasfilm, Cyrus R. K. Patell

Other titles forthcoming:
Leni Riefenstahl, Jakob Lothe
Jane Campion, Bernadette Wegenstein

CHRISTOPHER NOLAN

Filmmaker and Philosopher

ROBBIE B. H. GOH

BLOOMSBURY ACADEMIC
LONDON • NEW YORK • OXFORD • NEW DELHI • SYDNEY

BLOOMSBURY ACADEMIC
Bloomsbury Publishing Plc
50 Bedford Square, London, WC1B 3DP, UK
1385 Broadway, New York, NY 10018, USA
29 Earlsfort Terrace, Dublin 2, Ireland

BLOOMSBURY, BLOOMSBURY ACADEMIC and the Diana logo are
trademarks of Bloomsbury Publishing Plc

First published in Great Britain 2022

Cover image: *Inception* (2010) (© Collection Christophel / Alamy Stock Photo)

A catalogue record for this book is available from the British Library.

Library of Congress Cataloging-in-Publication Data
Names: Goh, Robbie B. H., 1964- author.
Title: Christopher Nolan : filmmaker and philosopher / Robbie B.H. Goh.
Description: London ; New York : Bloomsbury Academic, 2022. |
Series: Philosophical filmmakers | Includes bibliographical
references and index.
Identifiers: LCCN 2021025505 (print) | LCCN 2021025506 (ebook) |
ISBN 9781350139961 (hardback) | ISBN 9781350139978 (paperback) |
ISBN 9781350139992 (epub) | ISBN 9781350139985 (ebook)
Subjects: LCSH: Nolan, Christopher, 1970–Criticism and interpretation. |
Philosophy in motion pictures. | Postmodernism. | Motion picture
producers and directors–Great Britain–Biography.
Classification: LCC PN1998.3.N65 G64 2022 (print) | LCC PN1998.3.N65
(ebook) | DDC 791.4302/33092–dc23
LC record available at https://lccn.loc.gov/2021025505
LC ebook record available at https://lccn.loc.gov/2021025506

ISBN: HB: 978-1-3501-3996-1
         PB: 978-1-3501-3997-8
         ePDF: 978-1-3501-3998-5
         eBook: 978-1-3501-3999-2

Series: Philosophical Filmmakers

Typeset by Integra Software Services Pvt. Ltd.
Printed and bound in Great Britain

To find out more about our authors and books visit www.bloomsbury.com
and sign up for our newsletters.

CONTENTS

LIST OF FIGURES

ACKNOWLEDGEMENTS

Research on this book was funded in part by an HDRSS grant from the National University of Singapore. I am grateful for this financial support which allowed me to acquire the necessary material.

To series editor Costica Bradatan I am grateful for conversations, the exchange of ideas, comments and advice which have all fed into this volume.

The anonymous reviewers of the original book proposal and (especially) of the complete draft made many useful comments and suggestions which have all helped in the shaping of this book in its final form.

At Bloomsbury, Frankie Mace, Liza Thompson and particularly Lucy Russell were very helpful and efficient in their handling of this project, and I owe them my thanks.

To my Heavenly Father, as always, I am grateful for His love and guidance, and the way He inspires our philosophy, ideas, morals and culture – for 'in Him we live, and move, and have our being'.

1

Christopher Nolan as philosophical filmmaker: Themes, methods and influences

Introduction: Nolan's philosophical world view

Christopher Nolan as philosophical filmmaker is elusive, almost enigmatic. Starting out as a maker of Indie films (*Following*, 1998; *Memento*, 2000), he has gone on to helm large-budget superhero movies (his Batman trilogy of 2005, 2008 and 2012), historical movies (*Dunkirk*, 2017) and science fiction (*Interstellar*, 2014; *Tenet*, 2020). When *Inception* appeared in 2010, it generated a considerable amount of viewer discussion because of its ambiguities and layering of dreams-within-dreams; yet at the same time, Nolan considers himself a storyteller who does not want his audiences to watch his films 'in an overly cerebral way' (Berman 2017). For all the lauded thoughtfulness and detail in his films, the action sequences in films like *Inception* or his trilogy of Batman films can be as taut and fast paced as that of directors known only for action films, such as John McTiernan or Antoine Fuqua. A traditionalist of film technique who refuses to film in digital format or (as far as possible) to use CGI effects, he nevertheless favours filming in IMAX and believes that his films would be 'very conducive to converting to 3-D' (Resner 2012).

One of the most intriguing aspects of Nolan as filmmaker is the way in which he incorporates philosophical ideas into films in which suspense, action and even violence feature quite prominently. The contrast with such philosophical filmmakers as the Frederico Fellini of *La Dolce Vita*, or the Ingmar Bergman of *The Seventh Seal*, or the Henry Jaglom of *Venice/Venice*, is pointed. Great philosophical films grapple with certain broad philosophical themes in common – such as existential meaning, the morality of actions, the individual and society, appearance versus reality – and these make their appearance in Nolan's films as well. However, in terms of his ability to incorporate these themes into suspense films, the more appropriate comparisons might be with Alfred Hitchcock or Stanley Kubrick. Yet Nolan's films also have more elements of the Hollywood blockbuster – with large sets and large-scale action, and an abiding concern for keeping the audience engaged and enthralled – than the works of filmmakers like Hitchcock or Kubrick, but at the same time are more intentionally thoughtful and self-reflexive than the typical consumerist action film.

As difficult as it may be to categorize Nolan and compare his films with the work of any other single filmmaker, it is equally difficult to identify a single consistent philosophical thread or position running through his films. If Bergman's films are known for their 'ongoing dialectic' between 'death/absurdity' and 'life/meaningfulness', their theological atmosphere 'bathed in the Christian sensibility, rich in Lutheran overtones, that was the fruit of Bergman's upbringing' (Gervais 1999: 80, 81), it is much harder to identify a single philosophical strand that truly underlies Nolan's oeuvre. The philosophical concerns in Nolan's films are far more varied, lacking an easily identifiable signature theme.

On the surface, a likely candidate for Nolan's 'philosophy' might be the epistemological themes that feature prominently in a number of Nolan's films. In Nolan's very first film, *Following* (1998), redolent with Hitchcockian suspense and plot twists, the young protagonist follows the lead of a burglar (Cobb) and subsequently becomes involved with an attractive girl (the Blonde) and carries out a burglary and assault at their behest, only to find out that things are far from what they seem, with the truth hidden behind multiple layers of appearances. The theme of epistemic uncertainty comes to the fore in *Memento* (2000), where the protagonist Leonard, who suffers from anterograde amnesia, investigates his wife's murder and makes mnemonic devices out of polaroids, notes and tattoos. Without the ability to remember what transpires the day before, his quest for the truth based on very uncertain data that he constructs for himself, Leonard (like the Young Man in *Following*) is prey to manipulation by others for their own agendas and is also not above forcing the data into an interpretation that suits his own purposes. The uncertainty of knowledge and the evasiveness of truth appear among the themes of films like *The Prestige* (2006), which is about a competition between rival illusionists, and in the science fiction film *Interstellar* (2014), where data is made uncertain by the space-time disruptions of a black hole. Epistemology is central in *Inception* (2010), a thriller based on the premise of dream-manipulation and the possibility of dreams-within-dreams.

It is thus hardly surprising that much of the scholarship on the philosophy of Christopher Nolan has focused on epistemology and related issues of illusion, self-deception, memory and desire. *Inception*, especially, has come in for particular attention, its premises of dream-action and dreams-within-dreams invoking the philosophical thought of Plato, Descartes and Zhuangzi (Botz-Bornstein 2011: vii–viii; Wenmackers 2011: 8). The film's exploration of the possibility of planting an extraneous thought into the mind of another ('inception') while concealing the fact that it comes from someone else has provoked comparisons with William James's psychology of 'attention' and John Dewey's 'choice of action' (Testerman 2011: 68–9). The possibility of an inception (particularly in one's vulnerable dream state) raises related issues of choice and free will and even larger issues of individuality and the self (Fitzpatrick and Johnson 2012).

While *Inception* and its epistemology-related issues are obviously significant in Nolan's oeuvre, it would be a mistake to focus only on this film and these issues. A useful collection of essays, *The Philosophy of Christopher Nolan*, divides itself into four parts to address the major philosophical areas that the contributors see in Nolan's films: 'Moral Philosophy', 'Politics and Culture', 'Epistemology and Metaphysics' and 'Time and Selfhood' (Eberl and Dunn 2017). The sixteen essays in this collection also usefully cover a wider spread of Nolan films than just *Inception*, recognizing the philosophical thought interwoven into the whole corpus. Yet even these four categories cannot be expected to do full justice to the range of ideas and concerns in Nolan's films which also include (in addition to the epistemological, moral and political areas aforementioned) capitalist society (greed and inequality); language (intentionality, reference, speech acts); the relationship between art and truth (the representationality and reflexity of film); the relationship between the sexes (and the role of desire and love); and what might loosely be called 'faith' (belief that is maintained even in the absence of certainty, and which prompts action such as atonement and sacrifice), among others.

The overarching scheme: The condition of the individual in a postmodern market society

In addition to recognizing the wide range of Nolan's philosophical ideas, what is also required is a sense of the connectedness of Nolan's thought, the way in which his films speak not only to his audiences, but dialogically to each other as well. Nolan's films of the same period tend to explore a similar set of themes and ideas, which progressively expand and interconnect in the course of his career, so that the later films incorporate many of the individual philosophical ideas and themes in the earlier films, while also connecting them to a larger framework of thought. Without wanting to reduce or oversimplify this complex set of ideas, for the sake of wholistic understanding we might call it Nolan's vision of the condition of the individual in a postmodern market society. This vision raises a number of related philosophical concerns: the psychological and epistemic condition of the individual; the morality of the individual's actions in response to particular social conditions and scenarios; the psychology and morality of the individual's social (including familial) interactions; the ideology of the market and the role of corporations; morality in the public sphere; and the possibility of transcendent moral actions that escape the epistemic, psychological and moral bind of postmodern society.

Nolan's protagonists are often isolated individuals, psychologically complex, and often possess obsessive and narcissistic traits which make them prone to serious errors of judgement and rash actions that have grave consequences. These individuals function in a social setting – largely urban, capitalist, with contending interests and powers – where epistemic uncertainties find no objective truth and order, and where individual self-interests often collide violently. Ethics offers only a partial guide to such individuals, and many of Nolan's films feature a protagonist who, while admirable in many ways and possessing some form of ethical code, compromises that code in a key moment of his (since they are almost always male) career. The inner struggle of the protagonist thus plays out significant moral issues. The protagonist's career also puts him in conflict with others in society: either through conflicting political philosophies, or the conflicting morality of ends versus means, or in zero-sum scenarios where the individual has to choose between alternative actions which both have negative outcomes.

The protagonist's moral struggle is further complicated by the uncertainties of knowing and acting. Here language and narrative play a crucial role, and most of Nolan's films involve both narrative complexity as well as a philosophical awareness of the problem of 'language' (broadly understood to include verbal language, visual signs, symbols) as a system of reference. Nolan is known for the narrative complexity of his storytelling, for example in *Memento* which has two narrative strands, one of which moves in reverse sequence, or in *The Prestige* which tells the stories of the two competing illusionists Borden and Angier through different timelines and points of view (before converging near the end of the film), or the multiply embedded action sequences in *Inception*. Even the blockbuster Batman movies use multiple narrative flashbacks to create character complexity and tension before the final *denouements*. Modes of communication – letters, diaries, visual memories, symbols like the famous spinning top 'token' in *Inception*, devices like the Morse code communication in *Interstellar* – play a significant role in Nolan's narratives, calling the audience's attention to the ambiguous and often treacherous nature of language and meaning. There is thus a self-reflexive quality in all of Nolan's works, the film calling attention to the possibilities of misdirection and miscommunication in language, including its own filmic communication to audiences. This is not just self-indulgent narrative complexity for its own sake: for Nolan, the uncertainties of language and communication are part of his sociopolitical view, contributing to the epistemic uncertainty of individuals and thus also the political conflicts between individuals and groups.

These qualities of linguistic uncertainty, epistemic doubt, moral contradiction and political conflict seem collectively to create a characteristically postmodern, cynical ethos. Indeed it is not difficult to re-cast many of Nolan's philosophical issues into the established terminology of poststructuralism and Marxism-inspired cultural theory: epistemic uncertainty as the 'alienating' effect of 'false consciousness', moral struggle as the inherent 'contradiction' of capitalist society, political conflict as 'class struggle', corporate culture as the 'exploitation of the masses', linguistic uncertainty as 'language games', narrative ambiguity as *'aporia'*, and so on. In such a view,

Nolan would be seen as a 'postmodernist' filmmaker, presenting a 'pastiche' of contemporary styles and tropes, favouring 'decentered narratives' whose ambiguities avoid confronting the truth of the individual's position in society (Jameson 2003: 16, 23). Indeed, Nolan is often grouped together with 'postmodernist filmmakers' like the Coen brothers, Wes Anderson and Quentin Tarantino, on the basis of a perceived shared 'emphasis on pastiche', in contrast to the more 'modernist' sensibility, 'hewing to intellectual convictions' and 'moralism', of filmmakers like Aki Kaurismäki, Michael Hanneke and Lars von Trier (Nestingen 2013: 21–3). Nolan's use of peculiar narrative structures which play with time, order and causality is another feature which begs comparison with a postmodernism in which 'priority [is] given to the surface level of the style and the pastiche of generic conventions', and also identified in the works of Ridley Scott, Quentin Tarantino and Gary Ross among others (Flisfeder 2017: 101).

Without denying the postmodern qualities present in Nolan's films, to see him merely as a postmodernist filmmaker is to overemphasize such qualities at the expense of others and to miss the 'intellectual convictions' and 'moralism' (in Nestingen's terms on Kaurismäki, 2013: 21) that run through Nolan's thought as a whole. Nolan is no doubt a proponent of subtle and complex narratives that may be open to competing interpretations, but this is by no means to say that he seeks ambiguity for its own sake. Thus we have Nolan quoted as saying:

The only way to be productively ambiguous ... is that you have to know the answer for you – but also know why, objectively speaking. If you do something unknowable, there's no answer for the audience, because you didn't have an answer. It becomes about ambiguity for ambiguity's sake. There has to be a sense of reality in the film.

(Lewis-Krause 2014)

This 'sense of reality' in Nolan's films seeks to convey a vision of the fundamental reality of our postmodern society and the condition of the individual within it. This vision is no doubt complex and layered, rather than being presented in any tendentiously moralizing fashion, but it exists as the philosophical core of all of Nolan's films.

That moral, reiterated and dialogically developed over his corpus of films, has elements of a spiritual conviction, a tenet of faith. Despite their postmodernist elements, their depiction of epistemic uncertainty and moral conflict and compromise, many of Nolan's films incorporate (to varying degrees) a form of moral affirmation, a hope in human nature. The postmodernist elements of the films and the cynical world view they invoke do not offer fertile ground for a moral affirmation, and this is no doubt part of the reason that the 'postmodernist' view of Nolan as filmmaker has tended to stick. Some of Nolan's protagonists come to a bad end, overwhelmed by their struggle against moral corruption without and within. One example is Will Dormer in *Insomnia*, a detective who struggles with the means-versus-ends moral calculus ubiquitous in Nolan's films and who interferes with the investigation of the shooting of his partner in order to protect his own career and the conviction of all the criminals he has put away. Yet even in a film where the protagonist ultimately succumbs to the weight of moral compromises and cynicism, there is a moral affirmation in the bond that grows between Dormer and Burr, in the hope represented both by Dormer's act of coming to

Burr's rescue, and his preservation of her own moral integrity at the risk of his own reputation and legacy.

In other Nolan films, with a similarly dominant atmosphere of uncertainty and deceit, betrayal and compromise, the affirmative note comes in the form of 'love' (not just the romantic love between couples, but also that of the father for his children, or the individual for his community), the courage of ordinary individuals against overwhelming odds (an especially resonant Nolan theme), the belief that a truth will ultimately emerge even out of unreliability and immorality, and the redeeming act of sacrifice. Some of this moral affirmation has a pragmatic element resembling Jeremy Bentham's Utilitarianism, where moral action is depicted as the rational choice when the individual's interests are weighed against the greater good – a pragmatism which (the films are keen to emphasize) does not make the decision, and the sacrifice of the individual's interests, any easier. Simplistic Utilitarian considerations often prove to be unhelpful or inadequate in guiding the individual, and this is where Nolan (going against the postmodern cynicism prevalent in much of his work) seems to turn to transcendent moral ideas as might be found in the moral philosophy of Plato, Immanuel Kant, and Søren Kierkegaard, or even in Christian thought. When Nolan's protagonists or other characters make hard moral choices even in the face of material evidence and societal influence to the contrary, there is a deliberate and almost defiant quality to that morality which seems to invoke Kierkegaard's 'leap of faith' or Kant's 'good will', as well as religious ideas of sacrifice, redemption and atonement.

The moral affirmation is more evident in Nolan's later work, the popular, blockbuster films such as the Batman trilogy and *Dunkirk,* or the science fiction-cum-spy thriller *Tenet*. In many of his earlier films, morality is complicated and even obscured by Nolan's signature features of narrative complexity and epistemic uncertainty, and his characteristic view of individuals as deeply conflicted. Nevertheless the moral strand is still evident in these films, forming a continuity of thought in his oeuvre as a whole. We might thus say that Nolan is an epistemological/linguistic postmodernist, but a modernist and even an idealist in his (struggling, evanescent) invocation of a transcendent morality. The gap between those two positions is a significant one, and the different ways in which each film negotiates that gap are what makes Nolan such a fascinating and complex filmmaker.

Nolan as *auteur* – film and/as philosophy

The filmic treatment of that philosophical gap is the essence of Nolan's craft as visual storyteller. There are films – minimalist in action and mise en scène, with linear narratives and in an approximation of real time – where the philosophical thought is conveyed largely in the dialogue, for example Richard Linklater's *Before* trilogy or Louis Malle's *My Dinner with Andre*. Nolan's films – with their complicated narratives, suspense, fast-paced and often large-scale action – are very different from such (what we may term) 'philosophical discussion' films, instead evoking philosophical concepts through a combination of utterances, plot, narrative structure, symbolism, camera techniques and other film elements. This complex interweaving of different film elements to evoke philosophical thought is what gives Nolan's films their at times open-ended, ambiguous quality, since what is conveyed through one dimension of the film (e.g. plot) often seems to run contrary to or contradict another (e.g. symbolism). It could be said that Nolan hides philosophical thought – and in particular, his own characteristic philosophical position or outlook – within the complex warp and weft of the different strands of his filmmaking art. This is also what allows him to try to reconcile the two different *Weltanshauungen* of postmodernist cynicism and modernist idealism, of doubt and morality. It should also be pointed out that this layered philosophical message, expressed through different aspects of the film, is what makes his films – even the ones that seem on the surface to be relatively simple action films – worthy of much more detailed study.

Nolan is able to create this philosophical fabric in his film in part because of his involvement in many aspects of the film process. The term '*auteur*' has been used to describe directors whose 'force of … personality and unique obsessions' express themselves consistently in their oeuvre, notwithstanding the collaborative nature of filmmaking and industry considerations such as the commercial viability (or otherwise) of certain projects (Caughie 1981: 11). The concept of the *auteur* has been problematized, as (among other things) a 'hierarchical distinction', an 'anachronistic' view of the 'romantic figure of the artist' that ignored conditions of film production, a concept that could not be sustained over the diffusive whole of an individual's body of work (Watson 1996: 136–7; Lackey 2019: 547–48). On the one hand, Nolan would appear to be an unlikely candidate for an *auteur* by this romanticized notion of the director as presiding genius. More than many other filmmakers his body of work seems to reflect a heterogeneity of conditions of production, from the ultra-low-budget *Following* basically made by Nolan and friends, to the big-budget Hollywood films of the Batman trilogy and *Dunkirk*. There is also a wide range of genres and settings, from the film noir of *Memento*, to the science fiction of *Interstellar*, to the three Batman movies made in the DC comic universe, to the historical settings of *The Prestige* and *Dunkirk*. Nolan's films show the diverse influences of, and have begged comparisons with, those of Alfred Hitchcock, Orson Welles, Ridley Scott, Stanley Kubrick, the Wachowskis, Steven Spielberg, Quentin Tarantino and others – a diversity of styles that might trumpet his versatility but does not immediately suggest the consistent and dominant vision of an *auteur*.

On the other hand, Nolan's *auteur*-like qualifications consist in his knowledge of and attention to different aspects of filmmaking – with characteristic self-deprecation he refers to himself as a 'jack-of-all-trades' (Lewis-Krause 2014). On the majority of his films he is credited as both writer and director. He has also been executive producer for films such as Zack Snyder's *Justice League*, and producer or co-producer for most of his own films. He plays a very active part in post-production, including as editor of his early short films, and was also their cinematographer. In his later career he has worked with a consistent production crew, including his wife Emma Thomas as producer, his brother Jonathan Nolan as writer, and cinematographer Wally Pfister (Lang 2017). This consistency of crew, combined with Nolan's own broad background, has allowed him to pursue certain signature themes and stylistic features across his films, with the consistent film team working to realize that vision. Nolan is known to be adamant about certain film techniques, refusing to film in digital, preferring to shoot in 70 mm, disdaining CGI effects and instead shooting physical action sequences on multiple cameras – even going so far as to blow up a real 747 plane for his 2020 film *Tenet* (Myers 2017; Hynes 2018; Welk 2020). His use of something of an ensemble cast across his different films – Michael Caine, Tom Hardy, Christian Bale, Anne Hathaway, Marion Cotillard, Cillian Murphy and others have all appeared in multiple Nolan films, spanning different genres – also contributes to the sense of a consistent directorial vision, as if he were using these powerful acting presences to convey the same reality or meaning incrementally across his films.

There is enough evidence to suggest that we can speak of Nolan as *auteur*, not in any naively romantic way of a dominant genius with a single tormented vision, but rather in a structural sense of a committed filmmaker whose contributions to various aspects of his films (not least as director), and leadership of a team of cast and crew, are significant enough to impress upon his *oeuvre* a vision and consistency of meaning. Nolan is an *auteur* precisely in this pragmatic or structural sense, where the close viewer is constantly provoked to find in the films (beneath the star power and blockbuster action) 'the traces of the [filmmaker's] submerged personality' (Caughie 1981: 12, 15). Nolan encourages this deeper viewing (and re-viewing) of his films, by the use of complex storytelling structures that beg questions of sequence of events (questions that can only be answered by rewatching the film), by a suggestive use of symbolism and visual cues, and by the self-reflexive ways in which his films act as metaphors for filmmaking and the interpretation of meaning.

Nolan's filmic technique – the telling of a story through the interaction of narrative, dialogue, plot, character, mise en scène, visual imagery and symbolism, and other elements – is complex and will be discussed in greater detail in the following chapters. However, it would be useful to offer a schematic overview of his major philosophical concerns and how they are elaborated on in his films.

Overarching vision: The condition of the individual in a postmodern market society

Theme: The main philosophical question	Sub-themes	Filmic manifestation(s)
The individual: the psychology of the self, motivations and influences, determinism and the possibility of free will	• Past trauma • Impetus for actions • External influences • Self-deception	• Isolated protagonists • The doppelganger • Multiple/conflicting identities • Descents into dark places
The Other: the bases of the individual's relationship with others, and whether self-interest is reconcilable with the good of others	• Treachery and betrayal • Conflicting loyalties • Tension between ambitions and affections	• Failed romantic relationships • Intra-family tensions • Manipulative mentors • Professional conflicts and rivalries
The object: the role of money and possessions, the ideology of consumer society, and their influence over the actions of the individual	• Obsessive goals and desires • Poverty and inequality • Theft • Corporations and organized crime • Class conflict	• Camera focus on everyday objects • Criminal and gangster figures • Omnipresent and seemingly omnipotent organizations • Social decay
Epistemology: information in a postmodern world and its (un)reliability as a basis for action	• Fragmented and unreliable stories • Deception • 'Purloined letters' and lost messages • Misinterpretation	• Non-sequential narratives • Unreliable narrators • 'Found' documents • Intertextual allusions
Morality: the utility of the individual's actions, and the (im)possibility of avoiding negative consequences	• Cause and effect • Means and ends • Neoliberalism and democratic society • Sectarian interests	• Zero-sum scenarios • Dystopian landscapes • Copycat figures and social mimesis • Failure of authorities

To schematize Nolan's themes and filmic components in this manner is not to lose sight of the fact that Nolan's films work as whole experiences and not disjointed parts. There is clustering and overlap of his themes, and these in turn may be served by more than one set of filmic elements (just as conversely, one filmic element or signature technique may further more than one theme or sub-theme). Nor is the above table meant to be an exhaustive list of Nolan's themes, sub-themes and techniques, although it should serve as a useful schematization of his work and ideas.

It is worth reiterating that Nolan as philosophical filmmaker does not primarily rely on philosophical dialogue. Seldom, if ever, will his characters make pronouncements of great profundity or quote or paraphrase from major philosophers. There are no omniscient voice-overs or sage characters to serve as mouthpieces for Nolan's ideas. Instead, philosophy – in the sense of the provocation of reflection and thought on fundamental human issues in viewers of his films – is structured throughout Nolan's films. It is in the way in which the various elements of his films interact with each other – the narrative structure, characterization and characters' actions, what is said (and not said), plot, camera focus, mise en scène – to create provocative, dissonant and ultimately open-ended stories, that Nolan functions as a philosophical filmmaker. One of his signal achievements is to maintain this quality of provocative dissonance throughout the wide range of genres that he has tackled. We see certain consistencies of theme and technique in the early Indie-*noir* films *Following* and *Memento*, as we do in the big-budget superhero Batman films, in the sci-fi films *Interstellar* and *Inception*, in the historical fiction *The Prestige*, and the historical war drama *Dunkirk*.

The structure of this book

Given the consistency of some of Nolan's major themes, it would be tempting to organize this study around those themes and discuss the films inasmuch as they deal with the themes. The disadvantage of such an approach would be to lose sight of the development of Nolan's treatment of these themes over the course of his career, the ways in which he progressively expands on them and deploys new film elements to address these concerns. The other disadvantage of a theme-centred approach – in which the films seem to be significant only inasmuch as they convey some thought or idea – is also to lose sight of the films as films, the ways in which each one is constructed to tell a story.

Accordingly, this book will take a chronological and developmental approach instead, discussing the films according to periods in Nolan's career and showing how his treatment of certain themes develops over time. In this approach, we are greatly helped by the fact that Nolan's work can (without too much violence) be placed into phases, within each of which the films offer comparisons and contrasts fruitful for a study of philosophical ideas. This phased and developmental analysis of Nolan's films allows us to see more clearly the consistency of his primary concerns, even as he takes on new genres in the later phases of his career.

Chapter 2 examines Nolan's earliest films: *Following* (1998), *Memento* (2000), *Insomnia* (2002) and *The Prestige* (2006). Although the first of the Batman films, *Batman Begins* (2005), belongs chronologically in this period, thematically and in terms of genre it should be discussed together with the later two films in the trilogy.

In this first phase of his career, Nolan establishes his postmodernist ethos through his signature use of complex achronological narratives, his depiction of traumatized loner protagonists unable to connect with others in society, and his creation of a world view characterized by the lapse of social morality and authority. In this early phase, the influence of film noir on Nolan is clear and evident in his depiction of femme fatales and compromised policemen, and plots of treachery and betrayal. In this early phase, Nolan establishes the symbolism of the doppelganger and the psychological descent to evoke the unstable psychology of his protagonists and to raise fundamental questions about human motivation, will and choices, action, and moral consequences. These tropes and devices will also feature in his later work.

Chapter 3 studies Nolan's well-known and much-analysed science fiction films, *Inception* (2010) and *Interstellar* (2014). Again, films in the Batman trilogy – the *Dark Knight* (2008) and *The Dark Knight Rises* (2012) – chronologically belong in this period, but the thematic gravity of the DC comics franchise and the big-budget studio production exert their own pull and impose their own coherence on the trilogy. With genre expectations very different from the *noir* and suspense films of his earlier work, *Inception* and *Interstellar* rework Nolan's early themes and techniques into the conventions of science fiction such as quantum indeterminacy, global apocalypse, technological enhancement and transformation of the human, and the traversing of different times and states. Science fiction's concern with dystopian states also allows Nolan to paint a broader social canvas than in his earlier films, which (with the exception of *The Prestige*) typically involve a handful of primary characters moving in a very limited social sphere. *Inception* and *Interstellar*, in addition to pursuing Nolan's concerns about individual psychology and morality, also develop his growing concerns about society: its failure of authority, the consequent rise of competing and conflicting social factions, and the pervasive influence of capitalist ideology. In this phase, Nolan's earlier concerns about individual psychology and free will now get placed in a broader social context where problems of right action have complex consequences for different social groups.

Chapter 4 studies the Batman trilogy together with the historical drama *Dunkirk* (2017), and the science fiction/spy thriller *Tenet* (2020). Here Nolan's focus on social issues is even more pronounced, certainly when compared to the minimalist social depictions in his earliest phase. The big budgets of these five studio films (and longer run times, when compared to the early Indie films) allow Nolan to depict a very broad social canvas peopled with different social groups, each with well-developed aspirations and anxieties, moral tests and choices. In this phase Nolan takes the trope of the zero-sum game (introduced in *Interstellar*) and foregrounds it as a central feature of contemporary society, the end result of the social failures and fractures depicted in the earlier films. Nolan's protagonists, forced to take action because of social failures, have to weigh the morality of different courses of action, the Utilitarian calculation of means and ends, none of which have easy answers. One of the most unique features of Nolan's interpretation of the Batman character is the complicated doubling of Batman and other characters, including villains like R'as al Ghul, Joker and Bane. This doubling reinforces Batman's and Bruce's moral dilemma in a postmodern milieu – a dilemma which may (or may not) be resolved by the trope of unselfish sacrifice that Nolan evokes in the trilogy and *Dunkirk*. The dilemma is also evident in *Tenet*, which in its use of science fiction premises – particularly the time travel that is at the heart of the film – clearly has similarities with *Inception* and *Interstellar*. Yet in its blockbuster action sequences, its broad social canvas, and its depiction of moral choice and heroism, *Tenet* is clearly a late Nolan film that shows similarities with the trilogy and *Dunkirk*.

The conclusion returns to the postmodernist ethos of Nolan's earliest films and juxtaposes this with the transcendent morality that might be the only way for the individual to contest the issues inherent in contemporary capitalist and neoliberal society. This transcendent morality – which arguably shows the influence of Plato, Kant and the Bible – may not necessarily be offered as a viable and comprehensive solution to individual and social ills. Characteristic of Nolan's style, the films make no dogmatic or tendentious assertion. Yet the suggestion of this transcendent moral idea, particularly in Nolan's late films, is undeniable and (again characteristic of Nolan) opens an intriguing dialectical space vis-à-vis the postmodernist and cynical world view that pervades his work.

2

The Dark Night: A discontented postmodernism

Nolan as postmodernist

In what seems an uncanny prescience, the protagonist of Nolan's early film *Following* – which appeared in 1998 – has a Batman symbol on the door of his flat. *Following* precedes Nolan's first Batman film, *Batman Begins*, by some seven years, at so early a stage of Nolan's career that he could not have foreseen his future involvement in the DC comics franchise. We might see this as the sign of Nolan's abiding identification with the 'dark knight', an emotional engagement with Batman's noir ethos and world view, functioning as the latter does in a society characterized by incessant crime, corruption and psychological conflict. Recognizing Nolan's affinity with Batman, we could refer to Nolan's noir world view as his own 'dark night' of the soul, a cynical world view that is in keeping with postmodernism's cynicism, its characteristic stance of 'decadence, relativism and irony' that stems from its Hegelian sense of the 'intellectual stagnation' of the present age (Bewes 1997: 31).

The scholarly view of Nolan as a postmodernist filmmaker is well established. Matthias Stephan sees Nolan's film narratives (particularly in *Memento* and *Inception*) as representative of 'literary postmodernism', which is characterized by 'rhizomic' structures, 'the use of techniques like intertextuality, metafiction, pastiche, playfulness, and the mixing of genres' (2019: 6). Similarly, Margaret Toth reads *Memento* as a postmodern 'pastiche' of '1940s classic noir', invoking but playfully subverting (in noir fashion) such tropes as home, nostalgia and memory, gender and masculinity (2015: 78–80). Others see Nolan's postmodernist genealogy in his *Alice in Wonderland* tropes of dream worlds and distorted-mirror realities, in the metafictional playfulness of his complex narrative structures, and in his use of various techniques of pastiche (Nestigen 2013: 21; Kayhan 2014: 37; McHale 2015: 53).

Nolan's undeniably postmodernist elements need to be qualified in three important ways: firstly, they are not merely confined to *Memento* and *Inception*, although these may be the films in which postmodernist elements are most clearly foregrounded. Postmodern themes and techniques are in fact found, in varying degrees, in all of Nolan's films. Secondly, Nolan's use of postmodernist tropes is not to the exclusion of other (and even contradictory) philosophical strands. Thirdly, Nolan's use of postmodernist techniques is not tantamount to a wholesale commitment to a critique of capitalist society and neoliberal ideology. While there are elements in his films that are critical of some of the apparatus of contemporary market society, and critique it in terms familiar to scholars of Marxist theory, it is important to note that the films are multifaceted, concerned with a number of issues concerning the general condition of humanity, and not limited either to a left-leaning critique of capitalism nor (conversely) to an unreflective echo of capitalist culture.

Nolan's body of work should not be conflated with the kind of postmodernist texts that offer a 'flat' and 'depthless' response to 'late capitalist society', a blanket rejection of the 'assumptions of modernity' such as state democratic processes and the 'unalloyed support for industrialism', the inescapable social 'discontent' that comes with the increased 'freedom' but also loss of individual 'security' in the present era (Aronowitz 1988; Bauman 1997; Jameson 2003). Nolan's films are too aware of modes of narrative and representation, too self-reflexive, to constitute this kind of uncritical echo and affirmation of our late capitalist ethos. What may be more helpful is Linda Hutcheon's understanding of postmodernism's 'complicitous critique', its ability to 'install and reinforce as much as undermine and subvert the conventions and presuppositions it appears to challenge' (1989: 1–2). While this paradoxical nature disqualifies postmodernism from any overt political statement or position, the postmodern text can retain the politics of a 'de-naturalizing critique', the work to '"de-doxify" our cultural representations and their undeniable political import' (Hutcheon 1989: 3).

Nolan is at his most postmodernist, not in any political positioning, but in his embrace of a poetics of poststructuralism which (as theorists like Hutcheon, Derrida, Lyotard and others have pointed out) contains an implicit textual politics, the 'de-doxifying' of assumed realities and conventional truths. In Derrida's words, the aim is nothing less than 'the liberation of the signifier from its dependence or derivation with respect to the logos and the related concept of truth or the primary signified' (1974: 19). This freeing of discourse from the confining assumption of a 'transcendental signified' (Derrida 1974: 20) was to emphasize that all meaning relies on discursive contexts, on 'supplementary' meanings, prior referents and interpretations (Zehfuss 2002: 239–40). Other thinkers have reinforced the understanding that our present society is inextricably bound to layers of mediation and re-presentation: thus Baudrillard, for example, observes that our consumerist society with its endless commodity choices is best described as a society of 'simulation', of the 'precession of simulacra' in place of the 'metaphysical' real object (1994: 2–5). Similarly, Lyotard maintained that after the horrific event of Auschwitz, what is no longer possible in social discourse is a sense of 'finite' meaning, instead of which we have a 'disjoining' of narrative, mere 'language games' (1989: 365–8). The liberation of the text from transcendent or metaphysical confines has also meant its liberation from any singular controlling meaning intended by the author, whose place is instead taken by an 'author function', an 'interplay of signs' (Foucault 1977: 116, 123).

A poststructuralist poetics accordingly foregrounds its own textuality through a series of devices that provoke reflection on language, authority, meaning, interpretation, the role of the reader/viewer and so on. The purpose of this self-referential poetics is not a kind of artistic self-indulgence, a withdrawal from social relevance or meaningfulness, although it is sometimes seen as such. Instead, this poetics is intended as a commentary on the power basis inherent in social discourses. As May (1995: 7) observes, 'for poststructuralism, the social field is a network of intersecting practices, each generating (by itself and in resonance with others) effects of power, power effects that are both productive and pervasive'. The purposefulness of a postmodernist and poststructuralist text is preserved in its interrogation or challenging of the 'effects of power' inherent in the social field, in its use of textual devices that discomfort or estrange the reader/viewer from an unthinking consumption of the text.

This discussion of postmodernism, while it cannot pretend to be comprehensive, is necessary in order to situate Christopher Nolan as (in some respects) a postmodernist filmmaker. Nolan's films – as a whole, and not just the oft-remarked *Memento* and *Inception* – employ many of the poststructuralist devices and themes used by postmodernist storytellers. At the same time, it is important to note that these postmodernist elements in Nolan's films are not merely for their own sake, are not artistic self-indulgence (or, even worse, stylistic bandwagon-hopping), but serve to convey a particular vision of society. As we will see later in our discussion, in order to convey that vision, Nolan ultimately has to qualify and control those very postmodern elements that he employs.

Nolan's postmodernist legacy is manifested in certain recurring features. Narrative structures are often complex, involving a non-sequential narration, comprising different segments including 'found' documents such as journals, reports, files and others. Plots often involve textual elements such as missing documents (or parts thereof), fragmentary bits of information or data, and equivocal or wrongful interpretations. Nolan, who studied English Literature at University College London, often shows his literary background through intertextual allusions, with references to Shakespeare, Dylan Thomas and other writers making their way into his films. Finally, and forming one of Nolan's key themes, characters (including those who narrate) are unreliable and often deceitful, with no omniscient-type voice-over to guarantee reliable meanings, or objective and reliable character to offer an objective and reliable account. Nor does Nolan's use of the camera POV lead audiences to a different and more reliable interpretation than that offered by the unreliable narrators. Nolan's predilection for the use of fixed cameras provides audiences with a characteristically narrow perspective, with relatively few roving or panning shots, replicating for audiences the kind of limited perspective and state of knowledge that his characters are experiencing.

In Nolan's early films – particularly in *Following* (1998), *Memento* (2000) and *Insomnia* (2002) – these postmodernist elements come together to create a world of fundamental uncertainty. Characters

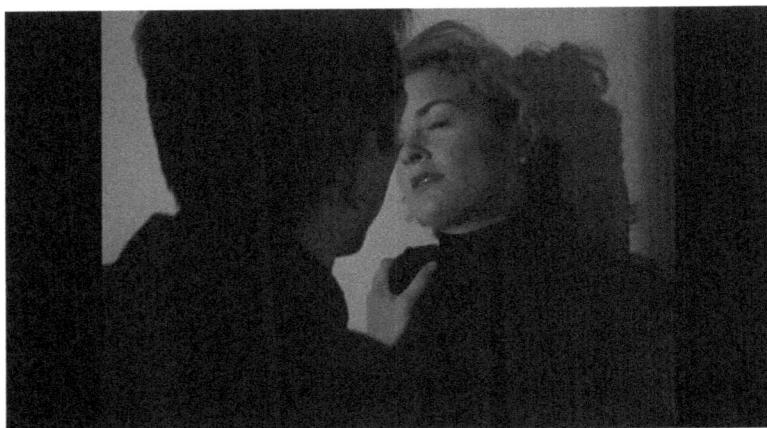

FIGURE 1 *Nolan's use of fixed camera positions, which results in shadows and offers limited audience perspective on characters (and for characters on each other), creating an atmospheric noir effect and also a narrow and particular focus that denies narrative omniscience and objectivity. Following (1998), directed and written by Christopher Nolan. United Kingdom: Next Wave Films.*

function in a world where they have to make decisions and take action based on unreliable information. The unreliability and uncertainty are pervasive and systemic, not episodic; they are seen to be inherent in the nature of human language, communications and discourses. Combined with Nolan's other foundational theme – the hidden depths and complexities of human psychology – the theme of unreliable knowledge creates a fundamental epistemic crisis, in which characters and audiences are forced to question what they know and how they can know it.

Flirting with noir: *Following* and 'unreliable objectivity'

If knowledge is problematic in the world of Nolan's films, it is also due to the fact that human nature is complex, contradictory, and possessing depths hidden even to the self. Nolan's use of film noir conventions in his earlier films thus allows him to evoke those complexities of character and psychology and marry them to what will become his signature structures of textual and epistemic uncertainty. Yet what Nolan creates in his early films is not so much a tribute or re-creation of film noir, as a postmodern caricature that uses noir conventions to depict a world of systemic deception and misdirection. Nolan's noir is not only about morally challenged characters and untrustworthy social relations, it is a commentary on the impossibility of knowing in a postmodern world.

Margaret Toth's assessment of *Memento* as a 'pastiche' of '1940s classic noir' (2015: 78–9) could also be applied in a general way to

Nolan's prior film *Following* – his first full-length feature, an Indie film that (without any pressure to conform to the commercial formulae and expectations of studio films) shows many of Nolan's stylistic and thematic roots. Both *Following* and *Memento* feature black-and-white footage, femme fatales, suspense, plot twists and other elements familiar from classic noir. Both films also feature two narrative techniques that Luhr (2012: 3) identifies as defining noir features from as early as Billy Wilder's 1944 *Double Indemnity*: firstly, there is a story told 'from its narrator's perspective, drawing us into his anxieties, moral failures, and feelings of entrapment'. Secondly, there is the technique to 'undermine suspense concerning the story's outcome' by the use of 'retrospective narration' and flashbacks.

In *Following*, a young man – a restless aspiring writer – takes to following random strangers in the streets of London, ostensibly to hone his skills as a writer, but (as it becomes clear in the course of the film) really feeding darker psychological impulses and needs. In this shadowy world of abandoned houses, seedy nightclubs, the sites of crimes and violence, the Young Man must undertake an epistemic quest that is also a psychological and moral one. He is taken under the wing of a man called Cobb (anticipating the name of Leonardo di Caprio's character in *Inception*), who initiates the Young Man into a form of burglary that is as much about the gratification of darker impulses (voyeurism, lying, the violation of privacy) as it is about profit. The Young Man's involvement with Cobb allows him to radically reinvent himself – he changes his appearance to correspond more closely with Cobb's, ditching his initial shabby leather coat for a nice suit, and gets used to frequenting nice restaurants using a stolen credit card given to him by Cobb – and also to get involved with a mysterious blonde woman. The Blonde manipulates the Young Man to break into the safe of a nightclub where she claims the nightclub's owner ('The Bald Guy') keeps compromising photos of her. In the course of fulfilling her wishes, the Young Man is surprised during the break-in and seriously injures a man using a hammer before making away with the photos and a considerable sum of money.

In a customary noir twist that is not too difficult for even first-time viewers to anticipate, it transpires that the Blonde is in a relationship with Cobb and is manipulating the Young Man at Cobb's request. Cobb tells the Blonde that he may be arrested for the murder of an old woman during one of his burglaries. The Blonde – in typical femme fatale fashion – uses her sexuality to entice the Young Man to break into the safe using Cobb's modus operandi, in the expectation that the police would pick up the former and interrogate him, thus weakening the potential case against Cobb. However, in a further twist that is not so easily anticipated, it turns out that Cobb is in turn manipulating both the Young Man and the Blonde, getting the former to help in the burglary of the Blonde's apartment so that her possessions will be found in his flat, and getting the latter to provide the blood-stained hammer with which Cobb kills the Blonde. It finally transpires that the Blonde had been blackmailing the Bald Guy over a murder which the latter committed at her flat, and Cobb – instructed to kill the Blonde – had undertaken the elaborate scheme so that he could kill her and direct suspicion to the Young Man instead.

Closer analysis of *Following* suggests that Nolan uses noir plot and mises en scène to question the nature of reality and experience. One technique he uses to this end is the focus on objects, a pseudo-objectivity that ultimately turns out to subvert any possibility of objectivity. Cobb, no ordinary burglar, teaches the Young Man to look closely at objects as a means of interpreting the character of the home's occupants. The camera is complicit in this, zooming in with seeming emphasis on details like books on the shelves of apartments the two men break into, the stolen credit card that the Young Man puts on the restaurant table, the objects (clock, dried seahorse, wad of currency notes) he takes home from the Blonde's apartment. Cobb teaches the Young Man to study things like books and CD titles and to look for the inevitable box of objects, 'an unconscious collection … a display'. This prompts the Young Man to steal the Blonde's box when he and Cobb break into her apartment, to display the box and her other things in his apartment, and to carry around in his pocket a strip of passport photos of her. The passport photos (apart from allowing the Young Man to identify the Blonde and shadow her) seem to link to the many photos of the Blonde in her apartment that the two men comment on and also to the nature of the mysterious photos in the Bald Guy's safe (which the Blonde tells the Young Man not to look at, saying that they are revealing photos of her, but which turn out to be innocuous fashion photos).

Other examples of objects highlighted by the camera's eye include the Blonde's piano (which dominates the Blonde's living room, and which Cobb tinkles on when they break into her flat); the piano bench (which the Young Man opens and rifles through, when the Blonde first invites him back); one of the Blonde's earrings (which turns out to be the item the Young Man is looking for in the piano bench, and which Cobb had earlier taken from her dresser and seemingly hidden among the music sheets in the bench); and the Young Man's hammer, which he is seen deliberately handling and experimentally tucking into various positions in his trousers before he breaks into the Bald Guy's bar, and which echoes the hammer which the Bald Guy uses to maim and kill one of his creditors. Even the Young Man is defined and characterized by objects: his shabby apartment is dominated by a typewriter, echoing the Blonde's living room which is dominated by the piano. Cobb unites both objects by tinkering on the keys of both of them in turn during his burglaries (which turn out to be pseudo-burglaries, since the Blonde knows that the burglary of her flat is part of the plan to implicate the Young Man, and the Young Man is the one who instigates the burglary of his own flat in order to validate himself in Cobb's eyes). The Young Man is also defined by his clothing: in the sequentially disordered narrative structure of the film, the only way to glean some sense of sequence is by looking at the Young Man's appearance and dress, whereby the unshaved appearance in the scruffy leather jacket signifies earlier events, while the suit and smart appearance signify later events, after Cob gives him the credit card.

This camera focus on objects will become a Nolan trademark, seen mostly notably in the spinning top and the child's pinwheel in *Inception*, but also in the top hats and the bouncing ball in *The Prestige*, the incriminating gun and bullet in *Insomnia*, the watch in *Interstellar*, and others. Nolan in an interview concedes a similarity between the spinning top in *Inception* and the famous example of the sled Rosebud in Orson Welles's *Citizen Kane*:

> And that is exactly the point – it's Rosebud, a visual symbol that sticks in your head from earlier in the story and then can take on new meaning later on ....

... Through the entire film, as you see his dependency on that symbol grow and through Ariadne's constant questioning of him, I think we start to understand that the whole reason he needs to spin the top at the beginning is because he's lost his own sense of what's real and what's not.

(Capps 2010)

Nolan's films tease with this seeming objectivity of the object – what we might call a strategy of 'unreliable objectivity'. As Lewis-Kraus (2014) observes, Nolan's films build a 'thick quotient of reality' as part of his depiction of 'people doing their best to get back in touch with consensus reality – against our tendency to be swept away by delusion ... or demagogy.' In *Following*, objects can indeed offer some anchor to reality – as when the audience pieces together the sequence by looking at the Young Man's attire – but they just as often lead one astray, as when the parallel between typewriter and piano suggests a personal connection between the Young Man and the Blonde, or when Cobb appears to place the missing earring in the Blonde's piano stool but has (unseen to the audience, but reported by the Policeman at the end) actually transplanted it to the Young Man's flat.

The other form of misdirection in the film is of course Nolan's use of a chronologically fractured, out-of-sequence narrative. The film opens with a voice-over dialogue (which, it will transpire, is the Young Man's confession to the Policeman after all the main events are over, including the death of the Blonde). The next few scenes show the Young Man, scruffily dressed, seeming to aimlessly follow random people in the streets. Next we see the Young Man dressed in a suit, watching the Blonde and clutching the strip of passport photos of her. Then the film switches to the Young Man in his scruffy leather coat again, following Cobb. The scene in which the Young Man lies on the rooftop, obviously in pain and retching with some pale object emerging from his mouth, precedes the explanatory scene later, where Cobb assaults him on the rooftop and stuffs a surgical glove into his mouth. Likewise, the Young Man searches surreptitiously in the Blonde's piano bench, before a later scene shows the audience the explanation that Cobb, while breaking into her flat with the Young Man, had seemed to place one of her earrings in the bench.

The misdirections of the camera's gaze on objects, and of the confused narrative sequence, reinforce Nolan's vision of a world of epistemic uncertainty, where the deviousness of human motivations is compounded by the unreliable knowledge to be derived from one's surroundings and circumstances. The Young Man's epistemic state demonstrates a mistrust of material reality that owes something to Plato, Marx and perhaps even St. Paul. As Brislin (2016: 203) says of Nolan's *The Prestige*, 'Like Plato's Cave, the ultimate staging of illusion of our senses, we find ourselves embracing shadows' – a statement that could easily apply to *Following*, with its conspicuous play of deep shadows (see Figure 1) and cave-like settings such as the basement bar where the Young Man first sees the Blonde and where he will commit his most serious burglary and assault. For the Young Man, unlike for Plato's philosopher, there is only the shadowy *kosmos aisthetos* or the world he experiences, with no possibility of seeing beyond this to the secure *kosmos noetos*, the world of ideas which for Plato was the only true reality. He (and by proxy the audience) is thus confronted with the question: 'How do we establish a "base reality" from which to make rational decisions if we cannot trust our senses?' (Brislin 2016: 204).

Following, ideology and influences: An early model of 'Inception'

The Marxist dimension of this untrustworthy material realm is suggested in the bourgeois aspirational nature of the Young Man's progression: the way he is willingly inducted or interpellated into what Cobb calls 'all this', the nice suits and fine dining, the power to take the Blonde on a date paid for with the purloined credit card belonging to a 'D. Lloyd'. His progression is thus redolent with Marxist ideas of bourgeois ideology, the myth that his new-found material possessions will confer upon him a secure (but ultimately illusory) identity and purpose. The scene in which he opens the Bald Guy's safe to find (in addition to the envelope of photos) thick wads of money which, lacking a bag, he then straps to his body with duct tape, is absurd in both a comic as well as an existential sense.

FIGURE 2 *The Young Man taping money to his body after breaking into the Bald Guy's safe. Following (1998), directed and written by Christopher Nolan. United Kingdom: Next Wave Films.*

While it is comical that the bar should not contain so much as a paper bag for him to carry the money away, the scene emphasizes the way in which money has encroached onto his own personhood and now (literally strapped like padding around his body) forms a buffer between that personhood and the rest of the world. In this world mediated by money that the Young Man has now entered, 'absolute knowledge' of objects recedes and is replaced by the 'value' that an object has for a user (Simmel 1978: 85, 109). Simmel's articulation of the abstract role of money nicely ties the mediating role of money to the similarly abstract nature of language:

> As a visible object, money is the substance that embodies abstract economic value, in a similar fashion to the sound of words which is an acoustic-physiological occurrence but has significance for us only through the representation that it bears or symbolizes. If the economic value of objects is constituted by their mutual relationship of exchangeability, then money is the autonomous expression of this relationship. Money is the representative of abstract value. From the economic relationship, i.e. the exchangeability of objects, the fact of this relationship is extracted and acquires, in contrast to those objects, a conceptual existence bound to a visible symbol.
>
> (Simmel 1978: 127)

Simmel's account helps us understand that for the Young Man, this sudden enfolding of his self into the world of money has epistemological and also ontological implications. Money, in being the 'representative of abstract value', stands between the individual and reality and causes the individual to view the world through a transformative filter: thus 'what we mean by valuation ... is something independent of this world; it is not part of it, but is rather the whole world viewed from a particular vantage point' (Simmel 1978: 62). Simmel distinguishes this abstract value of money from the 'specific phenomena of reality' which he associates with 'ideas, as with Plato and Schopenhauer, *logoi* as with the Stoics, the *a priori* as with Kant or stages in the development of reason as with Hegel' (Simmel 1978: 129). The Young Man's interpellation into the world of money and material things is also his loss of Platonic certainty, his descent into the 'below' world inhabited by worldly people like the Bald Guy and Cobb, where objects prove unreliable because they cannot be fully known, and their values change at the intersection of the changing values that people place on them. If this is a loss of Platonic 'ideas' (*noetos*), it is also a loss of the divine certainty, the fall into an order of transient and corrupting earthly values, spoken of by St. Paul and other apostles in the Bible (for example in 2 Corinthians 4: 18 or 1 John 2: 15–17).

In this latter, Biblical sense, the Young Man's relationship with Cobb can be seen as a kind of Faustian compact, a straying into a world that is both morally dubious as well as deceptive and uncertain. The Young Man, shown early in the film to be a blank slate without a stable identity of his own, is susceptible to the influence of others (persons and things), and Cobb takes full advantage of this to interpellate him both into material desires and criminal actions. There is a play on the title of the film, in various senses: not only is the Young Man literally following (or 'shadowing') others on the street, but the film's disrupted chronology also raises questions about order and sequence, cause and effect. By showing scenes of the Young Man watching the Blonde outside her apartment and on the street before the scene in which he and Cobb break into the apartment, the film confuses the conventional causality, suggesting that the Young Man's fixation with the Blonde somehow precedes and causes prior events such as the break-in, his involvement with her, and thus also her manipulation of him. This disordered film narrative serves to reinforce the film's view of human psychology, which is yet another play on the film's title. Anticipating the notion of 'inception' in the later Nolan film of that name – i.e. that thoughts can be planted in someone else's brain – *Following* is premised on suggestibility, on scapegoating someone by getting them to do what you want (without them realizing it). While film noir, dealing with crimes by the 'ordinary citizen' rather than gangsters, commonly deals with the manipulation and scheming which leads these erstwhile citizens into criminal acts (Fluck 2001), *Following* elevates the theme of manipulation by suggesting its ubiquitousness (by persons and things), that it is constitutive of the human condition.

The Young Man is manipulated not only by the Blonde, but also by Cobb and (behind the scenes) by the Bald Guy for whom Cobb works. The role of the Bald Guy (in terms of screen time, a minor character) in manipulating the Young Man is suggested early in the film, when the Blonde first points him out to the Young Man and then slaps the Young Man before walking out of the bar. The Bald Guy, seated apart from them at a table, laughs at this interaction: is this because he sees evidence of the Blonde's faithfulness to him in her humiliating rebuff of the Young Man's advances (as the audience may initially think)? Or is it because he knows that his own manipulation of the Young Man, mediated through the agencies of Cobb and the Blonde, has begun (as the audience may be more inclined to think by the end of the film)? Not only are the manipulators multiplied in this film, but so are the manipulated: even as the Blonde manipulates the Young Man, so is she also manipulated by Cobb. Arguably, too, the Policeman to whom the Young Man confesses is also manipulated, into viewing him as the only suspect for the Blonde's torture and murder.

The film foregrounds the process of 'inception' (to borrow the terminology of Nolan's later film), by showing how the Young Man's actions are preceded by suggestions, images and objects. Many of them expectedly come from his main manipulators, Cobb and the Blonde. Thus the scene in which the Young Man appears to choose a hammer as his weapon, experimentally tucking it into various parts of his clothing, is in a later (but chronologically prior) scene revealed to be the result of a suggestion by Cobb during a phone conversation. This suggestion is in turn in a later scene revealed to be the result of the fact that the Blonde is blackmailing the Bald Guy because the latter used a hammer to torture and kill someone in her flat. (In a bit of intertextual suggestibility, the scene might be an echo of the famous scene in Dostoevsky's *Crime and Punishment*, where Raskolnikov experiments with hiding an axe in his clothing, before using it to murder and rob two women.) The Young Man in an early scene is seen watching for the Blonde outside her flat, clutching a strip of her passport photos; only in a later scene is it revealed that he took the photos from her flat when he and Cobb burgled it, and the theft of the photos may have been implanted in him by Cobb's calling attention to her framed photos with the comment that she's 'a looker'. The film's narrative reinforces this notion of suggestibility, that action which appears to be self-willed (partly because it appears first in the film) is eventually (and in later scenes) revealed to be the result of suggestion or psychological implantation.

In the final analysis, the ubiquitousness of manipulation is brought home by the fact that the film has manipulated the audience as well. The viewer is complicit in the processes of manipulation, by accepting the narrative's precession of action only to be told in later scenes that these actions were planted by others. When the camera zooms in and lingers on an object – books on a bookshelf, the Blonde's face and her expression of thoughtful detachment as the Young Man kisses her, the object coming out of the Young Man's mouth after Cobb beats him up – the viewer is complicit in investing significance and possible meaning in these objects, in interpreting them in ways that (in most instances) turn out by the end of the film to be misdirected.

When the Blonde finally reveals the plot (as she understands it) to the Young Man, he threatens to go to the police: 'I'm going to tell them everything and they'll believe me, because it's the truth.' This of course proves to be heavily ironic: within the film's narrative structure, mise en scène and symbolism, 'truth' turns out to be as elusive as the figure of Cobb himself. After the Young Man's confession, the Policeman tells him, 'We don't know this Mr Cobb of yours,' indicating that Cobb's story to the Blonde – that the Young Man needed to provide a diversion to throw off police suspicions of Cobb – is a lie. The film ends with the camera's intermittent view of Cobb as shadowy figures in a crowd pass in-between; after one group walks past, Cobb has disappeared. He takes with him any possible account of his background, real identity, and even motives – he tells the Blonde just before he murders her that he has been commissioned by the Bald Guy to stop her blackmail, but he is never seen in the Bald Guy's company or even talking to him over the phone. His explanation to the Blonde could be yet another glib lie, like the earlier narrative he spins for the

Blonde, and the lies he tells the Young Man. Far beyond a film noir villain or ordinary citizen wracked by guilt and temptation, Cobb is an enigmatic, Mephistophelean figure, a depthless embodiment of the film's postmodern puzzles.

Memento: Amnesia and (self)deception as postmodern condition

In an early review, critic Andy Klein (2001) sums up the peculiarly enigmatic nature of Nolan's next film, *Memento* (2000):

> *Unlike* 'The Sixth Sense' and 'The Usual Suspects' – indeed, unlike almost every other celebrated 'puzzle film' in cinematic history – 'Memento's' puzzle can't be undone with a simple declarative explanatory sentence. Its riddles are tangled up in a dizzying series of ways: by an elegant but brain-knotting structure; by an exceedingly unreliable narrator through part of the film; by a postmodern self-referentiality that, unlike most empty examples of the form, thoroughly underscores the film's sobering thematic meditations on memory, knowledge and grief; and by a number of red herrings and misleading clues that seem designed either to distract the audience or to hint at a deeper, second layer of puzzle at work – or that may, on the other hand, simply suggest that, in some respects, the director bit off more than he could chew.

Yet the consistency of storytelling techniques and themes between *Memento* and *Following* suggest that there is intentionality and purpose rather than Nolan having 'bit off more than he could chew'.

Memento uses an even more complex narrative style than *Following*, shuffling together two sets of narrative sequences, one told in colour and in reverse order, interspersed with another story told in black and white and in chronological sequence. Within this complicated narrative structure, the plot is similar to the noir style of *Following*: a vulnerable protagonist (Leonard) manipulated by various people (including the femme fatale Natalie) whose motivations are not always clear, even to themselves.

In fact, the complicated narrative of the film is not that hard to read, especially on repeat viewing: as Tseng and Bateman (2011: 116) observe, the film offers extensive 'networks for filmic cohesion and filmic conjunction', such that while 'the storyline is, in fact, extremely uncertain', the 'surface cohesion' of the narrative sequences allows viewers to interpret the sequence of events quite easily. However, being able to piece together the actual flow of events does not mean that all questions (particularly those relating to human motivations and morality) are answered at the end of the film (and even on rewatching). As with *Following*, *Memento* creates an atmosphere of uncertainty – one might even say unknowability – that raises abiding questions far beyond the information that is provided, even in the reconstruction of the film's sequence of events.

The audience encounters Leonard as someone who has anterograde amnesia and cannot form new memories and is on a quest to find the man who raped and murdered his wife (and whose assault on Leonard created his condition). He relies on his own hasty mnemonics – notes to himself, tattoos, polaroids with added annotations – to keep track of each day's events. Even so, he becomes the victim of manipulators, chiefly Teddy (a corrupt policeman who has apparently helped

Leonard kill his wife's murderer but continues to enable Leonard's fantasy of finding the killer) and Natalie (the girlfriend of a drug dealer killed by Leonard, who uses Leonard to scare off her boyfriend's angry associates).

Leonard essentially represents (in rather violent and extreme form) the truth of the human condition that 'you lie to yourself to be happy, we all do it', as Teddy says. Leonard has in his possession a police file (given to him by Teddy) from which he has removed twelve pages 'to create a puzzle you can't solve', as Teddy explains it: 'You don't want the truth. You make up your own truth.' If it is true that Leonard has already caught and killed the real criminal, it is significant that he has not created a note to himself to record that fact: Teddy points to a mysterious polaroid that Leonard has in his possession, one which shows him smiling, shirtless and with what look like bloodstains on his body. According to Teddy, he took that picture of Leonard the day that they caught up with and executed the killer: 'See how happy you were?' Yet this polaroid, unlike the others in Leonard's possession, does not have a note explaining its significance. The most telling evidence that Leonard's quest is in bad faith is near the end of the film, when Teddy explains these truths to him, and Leonard (unable to accept this) writes down pieces of information that will deliberately turn him against Teddy and his account: he writes the line 'don't believe his lies' on Teddy's photograph, and the film closes with him screeching to a stop before a tattoo parlour where (courtesy of the film's backward narrative) we know he will get a tattoo of Teddy's car license plate to help him identify his wife's 'killer'. This final scene explains to the audience the opening scene of the film where Leonard (seen in reverse action) shoots Teddy.

Stripped down to this basic scenario – a man without memory, who gives himself a raison d'être by selectively recording information that will allow him to believe that he is searching for revenge on his wife's killer – Leonard would be an entirely repugnant figure, his handicap offset by the deliberate way in which he manipulates his own notes to himself in order to justify his killing of Teddy and other violent acts. The film, however, complicates this moral picture in a number of ways. Firstly, the moral judgement on Leonard is mitigated by having other primary characters like Teddy and Natalie who also lie and manipulate others in order to achieve their goals. Both have their own form of justification: Teddy says that he manipulates Leonard in order to help him, to make him 'happy' by giving him a purpose in life. Natalie justifies herself by telling Leonard that she is in trouble with her late boyfriend Jimmy's drug-dealing associates. Both commit morally dubious acts under the umbrella of those justifications: not only is Teddy at very least an accomplice in Leonard's murders, it is suggested that he profits from these acts (as he appears to set up the encounter between Leonard and Jimmy to get Jimmy's drug money). Natalie recognizes Jimmy's car when Leonard drives up to the bar in it but seems to condone Leonard's role in the disappearance of Jimmy by not confronting Leonard or reporting him to the police and even sleeps with him (suggesting her desire for him and for a change in her personal life). The sub-plot involving Sammy Jankis and his wife also involves manipulation and deceit: in this supposed story (which Teddy at the end suggests is actually the story of Leonard and his wife – displaced onto the other couple as another instance of Leonard's inability to accept the truth), Mrs Jankis who is diabetic tricks Sammy into giving her an overdose of insulin, believing that Sammy would either confess to faking his anterograde amnesia or be shocked into recovering his memory. The degree of moral culpability among these characters varies, with Mrs Jankis and Natalie arguably at the lower end and Leonard and Teddy at the higher end, but the multiplication of these instances gives weight to Teddy's claim that 'we all [lie to ourselves to be happy]' and dilutes the audience's focus on Leonard's culpability.

Secondly, as in *Following*, *Memento* reinforces the idea that one's actions are not truly one's own and belong as much to suggestions and influences from the outside. Mrs Jankis becomes obsessed with the idea that Sammy is faking because Leonard (on behalf of his insurance company) denies Sammy's claim on the grounds that his condition is 'not physical'. Natalie becomes interested in Leonard's story because Jimmy (who has been dealing drugs out of the Discount Inn where Leonard stays) had previously mentioned Leonard and his condition, which leads Natalie not only to get involved with Leonard but ultimately to exploit his condition and use him as a substitute for Jimmy in her life. The ultimate victim of these forms of 'inception' is of course Leonard himself, many of whose actions are planted as suggestions by others: he goes to the Discount Inn at Teddy's suggestion, he drinks the tankard of spit-tainted beer because Natalie offers it to him 'on the house', and – most egregiously – he confronts and kills Jimmy because Teddy sets him up to do it. Leonard even practises 'inception' on himself, giving himself false cues at moments that he knows them to be false, knowing that he will soon forget his self-deception and will simply act on them as if they were true. The most telling instance of this is at the end of the film, when Leonard – unable to bear the truth that Teddy has just told him – leaves himself the clues that will ultimately cause him to kill Teddy. Leonard's form of self-'inception' thus validates Teddy's earlier comment to Leonard: 'You don't know who you are.' Even when Leonard recites his name and occupation, Teddy says, 'That's who you were, not who you've become,' pointing to the ways in which suggestions – even self-planted ones – ultimately change our nature and identity.

Thirdly, as in *Following*, Nolan once again uses objects (and the camera's gaze on them) to suggest their importance, while undermining that importance to pull the rug out from under the protagonist and audience. The parallel, here, between Nolan's two early films is telling. Like the Young Man, Leonard also goes from scruffily dressed (in a flannel shirt and down vest, and driving a truck) to well dressed (in Jimmy's suit and driving his Jaguar). Just as the Young Man takes a number of items from the Blonde's flat and places them around his own dwelling, so does Leonard carry around

FIGURE 3 *Leonard arranging his wife's belongings in an attempt to (re)create her memory and his identity with her. Memento (2000), directed and written by Christopher Nolan. USA: Newmarket Capital Group, Summit Entertainment, Team Todd, I Remember Productions.*

a bag of his wife's belongings and places them around his motel room (in one scene paying a prostitute to simulate his wife's presence) as a futile proxy for the life that he no longer has with her.

One object – a wooden table clock – even seems to be identical, or at least very similar, in both films, perhaps suggesting the universality of this material dependence within the human condition. In the Young Man's case, he changes his appearance following a suggestion from Cobb, although it is hard to be sure that some desire on his part – to appear more attractive to the Blonde, to sample the quality of life not possible to an unemployed writer – does not also factor in. In Leonard's case, stealing Jimmy's clothes, car and money has no connection with his quest for revenge and thus cannot arise out of that idée fixe. Like the Young Man, Leonard may have succumbed to the allure of material possessions and how they shape a certain identity for him.

The adoption of these objects, like the carrying around of his wife's belongings or the constant mental flashbacks to things like the insulin bottle or the electrified metal shapes in Sammy Jankis' memory test, seems to be a recognition that objects are 'an unconscious collection' or 'display' of personality and identity, as Cobb tells the Young Man in *Following*. If Leonard insists that 'I have to believe in a world outside my own mind', then it is material things to which he turns in order to try to anchor and give significance to that world. Unfortunately, that significance is not necessarily objective and a priori to the individual but can be invented or implanted, can be a memento of a real past or a false clue altogether. Thus the oft-seen insulin bottle turns out (by the end of the film) to be both true and false: it transpires (according to Teddy) that it does have significance, but as part of Leonard's story, and not that of Sammy Jankis. Conversely, Jimmy's suit and car have no significance to Leonard's quest and are in fact a false clue as to his identity, but they become adopted into his persona (and associated with him in the audience's mind, by virtue of the backward narrative), so that Natalie not only recognizes them but also accepts their new possessor, Leonard, as a kind of substitute for Jimmy. Objects, for Nolan, are indeed highly significant to individuals, invested with all kinds of emotional and psychological importance; unfortunately, the significance and interpretation of each one is unreliable. Personality, in Nolan's world, is not a given but is put on and acquired much the way we acquire objects in a consumerist world. In Platonic terms, personality is 'becoming' and not 'being', unstable and in transition rather than fixed, thus reinforcing Teddy's words to Leonard: 'That's who you were, not who you've become.'

If personality is thus protean and 'becoming', then the attribution of moral agency for any particular action becomes problematic. *Memento* (again resembling *Following*) disrupts our moral sense by disrupting sequence and causality. By reversing the sequence of events, *Memento* fosters a habit of suspension of judgement in the audience, of waiting for the prior events (which come later in the film's disordered sequence) to explain later ones (which the audience sees earlier). Thus the viewer sees Leonard shooting Teddy at the very beginning of the film but does not get an explanation (even if only a morally ambiguous one, at best) of this until near the end of the film. For the majority of the film we see Leonard dressed nicely in a suit and driving a Jaguar, and again it is only near the end of the film that this picture of seeming affluence is punctured with the scene of Leonard putting on Jimmy's clothes and stealing his car. Another version of narrative 'inception' takes the form of what appear to be mental flashbacks to scenes involving Leonard's wife Catherine, in particular the oft-repeated image of her suffocating on the bathroom floor with a plastic bag over her head. Rather than coming at the beginning of the film to give audiences a clear moral guide on following events, these images are interspersed through the film, almost as if they are a retroactive justification for Leonard's actions rather than their prior cause. The images of Catherine Shelby are further complicated by Teddy's account near the end of the film, that she in fact survived the assault and instead died because Leonard gave her an insulin overdose – again, an instance of narrative 'inception' where the death of Catherine in the assault and Leonard's quest for revenge are planted in the audience as 'facts' before Teddy's alternative explanation near the end.

Camera focus, mise en scène and narrative structure thus combine to interpellate the audience into a world where actions seem to 'precede' causal explanations, where ostensible causes may later turn out to be implanted or are otherwise just misdirections, where personality itself is not stable and continuous but suggestible and malleable. The world of *Memento* is one in which (as Natalie says) 'you can question everything, you can never know anything for sure'. In its reverse narrative (at least in the colour scenes), *Memento* bears resemblances to other reverse narrative texts, for example in Martin Amis's novel *Time's Arrow* or the film *Irreversible* directed by Gaspar Noé, where the reverse presentation of effect and cause results in a questioning of not just causality but also culpability and responsibility. Such texts may reflect a growing sense of 'causal agnosticism' in contemporary society, a 'diffusion of causality and responsibility' for increasingly complex and systemic social problems (Goh 2008: 15). In Nolan's two early full-length films, the exploration of causal agnosticism is an early articulation of his vision of a world in which human agency is severely qualified by materialism, corrupting social influence, social fragmentation and uncertain knowledge. It is also Nolan's early statement of a moral problematic, one which he develops in later films, together with a vision of its possible amelioration.

Insomnia: Doubling, descent and corruption

After Nolan's first two full-length features, where the clustering of themes and film techniques is clear, the subsequent films are less clear in terms of chronological grouping and thematic clustering. *Insomnia* (2002) followed after *Memento* and continues some of Nolan's themes of the tormented and morally riven protagonist in a world void of epistemic uncertainty. However, *Insomnia* lacks the convoluted narrative structure of the earlier two films and also has more of a fully fleshed and sympathetic protagonist than either the flatly naive Young Man or the dangerously protean Leonard Shelby. After *Insomnia* comes the blockbuster *Batman Begins* (2005), with quite a different film premise, being set in the DC Comics universe and employing far more spectacular sets and effects than Nolan had hitherto used.

The better comparison with *Insomnia* is thus the next film after *Batman Begins*: the 2006 *The Prestige*, a historical fantasy about the lifelong feud between two magicians. *The Prestige* picks up some of the themes introduced in *Insomnia*: protagonists riven between ambition and guilt, dubious decisions and actions that may be understandable to the audience but are also reprehensible, and a final attempt at redemption that is complicated and only partially effective. Both *Insomnia* and *The Prestige* also bring to the fore a theme that was hinted at in earlier Nolan films: the idea of the doppelganger, seen in vestigial form in the Young Man/Cobb pairing as well as in Leonard's echoing of different elements of Teddy, Sammy Jankis and Jimmy. The doppelganger, as a mirror of the protagonist, exposes dark elements which the protagonist is not otherwise willing to confront. In typical Nolan postmodern fashion, this mirroring also becomes a mise en abyme, a seemingly infinite regression which precludes any stable objective point outside of this, from which to derive truth or effect change.

Insomnia, in generally chronological fashion, tells the story of Will Dormer, a Los Angeles detective who is sent with his partner Hap Eckhart to the town of Nightmute, Alaska, to track down the killer of a young girl, Kay Connell. Dormer and Eckhart have an Internal Affairs investigation hanging over them, and Eckhart tells Dormer that he is going to 'cut a deal' in order to protect himself and save his career. A young Nightmute police officer, Ellie Burr, who hero-worships Dormer and has studied his cases, is assigned to assist them. In a stakeout on a foggy beach, Dormer shoots Eckhart while in pursuit of the killer, and the dying Eckhart believes that the shooting was on purpose, to stop him from speaking to Internal Affairs. Dormer identifies Walter Finch, a writer of detective mysteries, as Kay's killer, and in the course of the investigation Finch tries to enlist Dormer (through blackmail, having seen Dormer shoot Eckhart on the beach, and through persuading Dormer about the essential similarities between the two of them) to misdirect the investigation towards a scapegoat, Kay's ex-boyfriend Randy. Burr finds out the truth about

Dormer shooting Eckhart and also discovers evidence that Finch had killed Kay and is disarmed and about to be killed by Finch, when Dormer arrives on the scene. Dormer and Finch fatally shoot each other, and Burr (after confronting Dormer about the Eckhart shooting) is about to throw away the evidence that would incriminate Dormer, when the latter stops her from doing so just before he dies.

The film is Nolan's remake of a 1997 Norwegian film of the same name, but whereas the protagonist in that film, Jonas Engstrom, is 'thoroughly corrupt' and the film ends with his concealment of his role in his partner's death (Garcia 2006: 85), Nolan's remake focuses on moral ambiguity and shades of grey. There are some familiar Nolan storytelling features that complicate knowledge and judgement, both for characters as well as for audiences. The film overall makes ironic the Nightmute chief's comment early in the film: 'I think you'll find it's a lot more straightforward up here. Good guys, bad guys, and a lot less public relations.' The film uses the trope of insomnia to complicate the protagonist's mental state and point of view. Unable to sleep partly because of the midnight sun effect of summer in Alaska and perhaps also because of guilt, together with what appears to be an unusually empathetic ability that makes him a legendary detective, Dormer (his name an ironic play on 'dormir', to sleep in French and other Romance languages) experiences intra-scene flashes that resemble those that Leonard Shelby has of his wife. Looking at the cadaver in the morgue, Dormer sees flashes of the victim struggling and then someone washing her hair. Later in his hotel room, when he puts a picture of Kay (taken from his visit to her home) on the nightstand, there are intra-scene flashes of Kay laughing, with her hands up to cover her mouth. After the shooting of Eckhart, when Dormer is back in his hotel room, there is a flash of him picking up a revolver dropped by Finch, which (in the present time) he now hides under the floorboards of his hotel room. As his insomnia-induced delirium worsens, there are flashes to Eckhart holding a gun and in motion, Eckhart shot and dying, Kay laughing. Mixed up in these recurring flashes are two mysterious images: blood soaking into white fabric and a man in a suit seen partially in a mirror, washing or rubbing a red-stained white garment. These last two images also occur right at the beginning of the film, even before we are introduced to Dormer and other characters, so that they initially float around ('Rosebud' fashion) without being associated with Dormer's thoughts or with the actions of any other character.

These flashes also prove to be unreliable, although not to the same degree and in the same manner as Leonard Shelby's. It is never explained how Dormer seems to have flashes of Kay when he never meets her before her murder, and even before he meets Finch. Later when he and Finch meet on the ferry, and Finch confesses some details of his actions to Dormer, there is the same flash (of Kay laughing and putting her hands to her mouth) as Finch speaks that we see early in the film when Dormer is in his hotel room unable to sleep. We thus do not know whether or not the earlier flash is actually a glimpse into Finch's mind, even though the audience at that point has not been introduced to Finch and even though the camera POV suggests that we are actually seeing into Dormer's mental state. The mysterious images of the blood soaking into the white garment and the man in a suit partially glimpsed in a mirror are later explained when Dormer confesses to the hotel receptionist Rachel that he had planted evidence (in an earlier case) in order to convict a paedophile

FIGURE 4 *Repeated sequence of blood soaking into white fabric, and a man indistinctly glimpsed in a mirror, later resolving into an image of Dormer planting evidence to convict the paedophile murderer, Dobbs. Insomnia (2002), directed by Christopher Nolan. USA: Alcon Entertainment, Witt/Thomas Productions, Section Eight, Insomnia Productions, Summit Entertainment.*

murderer, Dobbs. The image of the man in the mirror segues into a clear image of Dormer planting the victim's blood, as he describes it to Rachel.

Yet Dormer's state of mind, like Leonard's, is unstable. After Eckhart dies, Dormer (in an echo of Shakespeare's Macbeth, who is also an insomniac and who sees the ghost of Banquo whom he had murdered) seems to see Eckhart among the Nightmute residents moving through the forest looking for evidence. When Dormer is shot by Finch and dying, Burr asks him if he had meant to shoot Eckhart to silence him, and Dormer's reply is telling:

> I don't know any more. I couldn't see him through the fog, but when I got up close he was afraid of me, and he thought I meant to do it. Maybe I did, I just don't know anymore.

The possibility that Dormer's self-incrimination is no more than an anxious response or echo of the dying Eckhart's fear and suspicion throws into doubt the epistemic value of flashbacks and memories. Just as in *Memento* we see images change as events unfold or other characters explain things to Leonard – such as the repeated images of Sammy Jankis giving his wife her insulin jab later transforming into Leonard and Catherine – so too in *Insomnia*, these flashes are difficult to attribute to a particular character's memories or POV and may also change and resolve, as the image of the man in the mirror resolves not into Kay's murderer but into Dormer from the Dobbs case.

Another Nolan technique for creating uncertainty is the technique of doubling, in which inception again plays a role in the blurring of boundaries between self and other. There are already suggestions of doubling in Nolan's earlier films: the Young Man clearly models his career on Cobb who is his initiator, he starts dressing like him, in a sense they both share the Blonde, and at the end the Young Man becomes the scapegoat for Cobb's murder of the Blonde. Leonard Shelby does a similar thing with Jimmy, putting on his clothing and taking his car and money and even slotting quite easily into the role of Natalie's lover. In another sense it is Sammy Jankis who is Leonard's double, a projection of Leonard's own struggles with his memory and troubled post-traumatic relationship with his wife. In yet another sense it is arguably Teddy who is Leonard's double, a Mephistophelean enabler who shares Leonard's ruthlessness and initiates him into a career of serial murdering 'John Gs', much as Cobb initiates the Young Man into the latter's life of crime.

The doppelganger is a staple of gothic literature, which Nolan the onetime literature student would have been familiar with. Famous gothic doubles include Jekyll and Hyde in Robert Louis Stevenson's *The Strange Case of Dr Jekyll and Mr Hyde*, Mary Shelley's eponymous Frankenstein and his monster, the also eponymous Dorian Gray and his monstrous portrait in Oscar Wilde's novel, and others. Webber's study of German romanticism notes the preponderance of the double figure as a sign of 'the dismantling of the idea of the transcendental subject', the depiction of 'subjectivity in crisis' (Webber 1996: 1). Various narrative modes of depiction of the double figure – as shadow, mirror image, libidinal self, transformed body and others – explore the central idea of 'schismatic identity', where the subject is no longer singular but dialectically divided into self and alter-ego (Webber 1996: 4–6). The trope of the double intensifies with modernity, with the political disillusionment after the French Revolution and the rapid socio-economic changes that led to an increasing sense of the 'alienation' of self from society, the growing sense of 'an internal and irreparable division in the individual psyche' (Botting 1996: 93). Sigmund Freud's theories of the 'unconscious' and the 'dynamics of repression' working to contain and conceal unconscious desires (Freud 1984a: 183–5) provided a psychological account of dividedness and splits in the self, allowing the doppelganger to be seen as a manifestation of conflicting aspects of the unstable self.

In *Insomnia* and *The Prestige*, Nolan's use of the double becomes both more explicit, and also more complicated, than in the preceding two films. Dormer and Finch are ostensibly on opposite sides of the law and morally opposite as well. Yet the trope of the flawed cop and that of the uncanny doubling between detective and villain are fairly well established in literature and film, seen in many of Arthur Conan Doyle's Sherlock Holmes stories, Martin Scorsese's *The Departed*, and

Kathryn Bigelow's *Point Break*, to name just a few instances. What is surprising about Nolan's treatment is not the fact that the policeman is fallible, but that he should be fallible in his very pursuit of justice, and because of the uncertainty inherent in the quest to uncover the truth. Nolan's casting of Robin Williams in the role of Walter Finch is part of this destabilization of assumptions about crime and justice, truth and falsehood. Williams, already known for his comic roles (e.g. *Mrs Doubtfire*, 1993, directed by Chris Columbus) or his roles as the manic and vulnerable protagonist (e.g. *The Fisher King*, 1991, directed by Terry Gilliam; or *Patch Adams*, 1998, directed by Tom Shadyac), is barely credible as a murderer. While over the course of the film he proves to be a formidable enough adversary, evading and manipulating Dormer and finally shooting him, Williams plays Finch as a sympathetic and even affable character (Lane 2002). He spends most of his interactions with Dormer trying to persuade him that he had not meant to kill Kay, that his relationship with her was not sexual, and that making Randy a scapegoat was justifiable because of Randy's abusive nature. Finch's approach to Dormer relies less on the blackmail that he saw Dormer shoot Eckhart (although that is implicit), than on the argument that he and Dormer are 'the same': essentially good (or at least ordinary) men who inadvertently kill.

The doubling between Dormer and Finch is done with characteristic Nolan subtlety, in elements of plot, dialogue and mise en scène. The boundary between Dormer's and Finch's minds is constantly blurred: even before encountering Finch, Dormer seems to see episodes that only Finch could have seen, for example Kay's hair being washed and Kay laughing at Finch. When Dormer and Eckhart finish viewing Kay's cadaver in the morgue, Dormer strokes her hair in an action reminiscent of the flashing image of a hand (presumably Finch's) stroking the dead Kay's hair as it is being washed. The film shows a progressive identification of Dormer and Finch, a subtle exchange of positionalities. While Dormer begins the film by tracking down Finch, later it is Finch who pursues Dormer, calling him at the hotel and even at the police station, setting up the meeting on the Ferry, relentlessly hounding Dormer to make him his co-conspirator in misdirecting the investigation towards Randy. While Dormer initially seems to be able to see into the killer's mind, later it is Finch who seems to be able to read Dormer, uncannily knowing the latter's insomniac state of mind and even his visions: 'Are you seeing things yet? Little flashes, tricks of light …. See your partner?' When Dormer finds and enters Finch's apartment, Finch's dogs strangely seem to be familiar with him, even licking his hand in welcome. Later after Dormer falls into the water while chasing Finch and returns to Finch's apartment, Finch knows he is there; Finch calls Dormer on his (Finch's) own telephone number, and Dormer answers it. At one point in Finch's attempt to persuade Dormer to help him, he eerily uses the same argument that Dormer had earlier used to try to persuade Eckhart not to cooperate with Internal Affairs: he reminds Dormer, 'Every one of those scumbags you put away will be back on the streets before you even go on trial.'

Another game of switched positions that Finch and Dormer play with each other concerns the .38 revolver that Finch drops on the beach and Dormer recovers. Dormer tries to plant the gun back in Finch's possession by putting it in the heating vent of Finch's apartment. During their ferry meeting, Finch suggests to Dormer that the revolver be used to incriminate Randy. Unknown to Dormer, Finch had already found the revolver in his heating vent and, when interrogated at the police station, claims that Randy has a revolver hidden in his (Randy's) heating vent. Dormer, opposed to making Randy a scapegoat, rushes to Randy's place to remove the revolver, except that it is not in the heating vent (Finch had hidden it in a barrel of motor oil), and Dormer almost gets caught trying to tamper with evidence. The ideas of using the revolver as planted evidence, the use of the heating vent (both as real hiding place and red herring), pass from Dormer to Finch and back again almost like in a mental game of tennis.

While the main doubling and inception take place between Dormer and Finch, there are other examples in the film. Ellie Burr, the idealistic young Nightmute cop, idolizes Dormer, telling him, 'I've *followed* all your cases' (emphasis added) – a verbal echo from Nolan's first full-length film, and likewise warning the audience that a certain unhealthy psychological dependence is at stake, as it was in the Young Man's 'following' of Cobb. Burr constantly quotes Dormer's supposed sayings and aphorisms back to him, even after she begins to suspect him of shooting Eckhart: 'A good cop can't sleep because a piece of the puzzle's missing, and a bad cop can't sleep because his conscience won't let him. You said that once.' In effect, she is using Dormer-inspired methods and values against Dormer himself – a process which Dormer encourages, for example when he refuses to sign her first report on the Eckhart shooting which is superficial and exonerates Dormer completely. He tells her to 'be sure of all your facts before you file that thing'. It is because of this mentoring and encouragement of Burr – performed perhaps even without consciousness or willingness on Dormer's part – that Burr continues the investigation and finally finds the shell casing. She associates the shell casing with Dormer again because of her zealous following of Dormer: she checks her notes on one of Dormer's cases and remembers that Dormer's back-up gun is a 9mm automatic (whereas Finch's .38, a revolver, would not eject its empty shell casing). There is even a scene where the psychological link between Burr and Dormer is established, similar to the ones that are shown to exist between Finch and Dormer: Dormer is seen slumped in his hotel bed, drowsy but unable to sleep, when the film cuts to Burr slumped in a similar position, drowsy from starring at crime scene photos and dropping off to sleep before she suddenly jerks awake with a sudden revelation about the shooting. Burr might be seen as a manifestation of Dormer's divided self, with one guilty part willing Burr to uncover the truth about the Eckhart shooting, but this is also to say that Burr in her hero worship of Dormer shows her own psychological malleability, her dependence on Dormer for her sense of self. This is true even after she discovers that he shot Eckhart: in the film's final scene, after hearing the dying Dormer's confession, she attempts to throw away the incriminating shell casing so that his name and legacy will be intact, and has to be physically stopped from doing so by Dormer.

If the complicated and overdetermining doubling in *Insomnia* problematizes the audience's sense of moral attribution, it also destabilizes the notion of the self as a discreet and comprehensible identity. Doubling in this film is reinforced by the trope of the descent into the depths, a spatial trope which was present (as a faint early trace) in *Following*, but which will be even more evident in later films such as the Batman trilogy, *Inception*, and arguably *Dunkirk* and *Interstellar* as well. Physical descents signal the psychological descent into the darkness of the individual psyche, the confrontation of truths about the self which may hitherto be hidden, uncomfortable, unacceptable. This symbolism of psychological exploration has commonly found spatial expression as a journey into the wilderness (Joseph Conrad's *Heart of Darkness* and the Francis Ford Coppola film *Apocalypse Now* inspired by Conrad's novel), a trial or ordeal (Jim Crace's novel *Quarantine*, Ron Howard's film *Into the Heart of the Sea*), or a life-changing episode (Brad Anderson's *The Machinist*, Robert Redford's *Ordinary People*), to mention just a few of many examples. Nolan's recurring spatial trope for psychological exploration is a descent into an unfamiliar lower place, often one that is dark and rough, and which catalyses a confrontation with a traumatic episode or memory. The correspondence with Freudian theories of the unconscious, and the conscious self's censorship and repression of 'instinctual impulses' (Freud 1984a: 186–90), is suggestive.

The clearest example of this in Nolan's oeuvre is the Batcave, which the audience first encounters in *Batman Begins* not as a shiny technological marvel (as in some of the other iterations of Batman), but as a raw fissure, wet and filled with bats, the scene of Bruce Wayne's childhood fall, and the source of his instinctual fear and adult psychological drama. However, before Nolan's helming of the Batman trilogy, he already introduced the psychological descent in *Following* and depicted it in complex ways in *Insomnia*. The Young Man's transition from his seemingly harmless observation of random people to his deeper entanglement with the Blonde is symbolized by his descent into the Bald Guy's basement bar where he first talks to her and also by the unusual architecture of the Blonde's apartment where the Young Man has to descend a flight of stairs to get from her door to the living room (which is not only the site of his entanglement with her, but also the scene of the Bald Guy's act of homicide). The descent suggests that the Young Man's entanglement with Cobb and the Blonde, his forays into crime, are also explorations of his own hidden desires and moral boundaries.

Dormer's psychological descent, triggered by insomnia and the stresses of the IA investigation (and later, Eckhart's shooting), is also symbolized spatially. When we first see Dormer he is on a plane flying over the Alaska wilderness, and shortly after this the pilot makes his descent to the town of Nightmute. An actual town in Alaska, the name comes from the Yupik word 'negtemiut', which means 'pressed down … people' or 'people of the pressed down place' (Bright 2004: 326). Dormer is literally pressed down when Finch escapes the stakeout by unexpectedly jumping through the floor of the beach cabin into a tunnel, and Dormer has to follow him through the wet and rough underground passage. It is shortly after this that Dormer shoots Eckhart, becomes convinced that he may have intended to do it, finds Finch's .38 revolver, and decides to frame Finch and tamper with the evidence. In his hotel room, he once again delves below the surface when he pries up a floorboard to hide Finch's gun. At the film's climax, Finch is holed up in a boathouse at his lakeside cabin and pins down Dormer and Burr at the main house with shotgun fire, but Dormer sneaks up on him by going through a trap in the main house and surfacing in the boathouse – an action that replicates the chase at the beach cabin, both in the descent as well as in the wet and rough passage Dormer once again has to navigate. Arguably another 'subterranean' site is the alley in Nightmute where Dormer fires Finch's revolver into the carcase of a dead dog in order to get the ballistic evidence to switch with the 9mm slug from his automatic that is in Eckhart's body. Although the alley is not a literal descent, its dark recesses and rough, wet floor are visual echoes of the passageway at the beach and lakefront cabins.

These subterranean sites literalize Dormer's descent out of his comfort level (so to speak) as a hero cop, trusted and respected by the likes of Eckhart and Burr, onto an unfamiliar level where his physical discomfort – stumbling and crawling down dark passageways, practising deceit in hiding evidence and having to dig out his slug from the rotting carcase of the dog – signals the psychological distresses he is experiencing. It is at this unfamiliar low sense of self that the doubling with Finch – something unthinkable to Dormer in his upright policeman's avatar – becomes insidiously plausible. Nolan's detective film, not a typical story of the machinations of a corrupt cop, becomes the enactment of the dissolving of one's rigid sense of self – a dissolution that is all too easy despite Dormer's good intentions. By depicting the insinuating power of verbal and conceptual 'inceptions', the worship and 'following' of one's heroes, the justification of means by ends, and the plausible similarities between oneself and one's antithetical double, *Insomnia* depicts Nolan's sense of the porousness of our sense of self and the fragility of its boundaries.

The Prestige: Rivalry, romance, and the unknowable self

After doing the first in the Batman trilogy, *Batman Begins* (2005), Nolan wrote and directed *The Prestige* (2006), which takes up many of these themes discussed above. *The Prestige* offers a version of the complicated narrative technique of *Following* and *Memento*, combining it with the theme of psychological descent and the symbolism of the double seen in *Insomnia*. It tells the story of two magicians, Alfred Borden and Robert Angier, who pursue an obsessive and intense rivalry that leads to pain and suffering to themselves and those around them. Their rivalry intensifies later in their careers over an illusion known as 'The Transported Man', which essentially involves the illusionist disappearing in one location and appearing in another. The Borden version, unbeknownst to anyone (but suspected by several), relies on the fact that there is actually a pair of Borden twins, while Angier's version relies on a miraculous machine custom-built for him by Nicola Tesla, which actually recreates an exact duplicate of the subject. Both acts require sacrifice: the Bordens both live 'half-lives' (as the surviving twin explains to Angier at the end), taking turns to be 'Borden' and 'Fallon' (the other twin in disguise, and serving in the capacity of engineer and factotum), with each twin also having to love one woman and pretend to love the other (the wife Sarah and the mistress Olivia). Angier's version requires him to murder the duplicate 'Angier' created during the act, each and every time the act is performed (and one of the final scenes of the film is of the abandoned theatre burning, with rows upon rows of water tanks in which drowned 'Angiers' can be seen floating). The plot device of the 'transported man' is thus a vehicle for Nolan to explore human obsession and the porousness of the self – both familiar from earlier Nolan films.

In *The Prestige*, Nolan returns to a more complicated mode of narrative than he employs in *Insomnia* and *Batman Begins*. As with *Memento*, the story is essentially told on two (or possibly three, depending on how they are counted) different timelines, although without the earlier film's reverse order: one is when Borden has been imprisoned for the supposed murder of Angier, and this is interwoven with flashbacks (as Borden reads Angier's diary) which tell the story of the rivalry and how Borden ends in jail, before the two timelines converge and we see Borden's conviction, execution and his revenge on Angier. However, even the earlier (rivalry) storyline is not told in chronological fashion: as Borden is reading Angier's diary, within that story Angier, in his attempt to discover the secret of Borden's transported man trick, is in turn reading Borden's notebook, which takes the audience even earlier back in time, to the beginning of the rivalry. The three timelines – prison, late rivalry, early rivalry – collectively do give the familiar Nolan sense of causal agnosticism or suspension, since the audience sees the consequences of the obsessive rivalry before becoming informed about its origins and causes.

There are also familiar Nolan devices to highlight epistemic uncertainty, deception (including, as always, self-deception) and problems of meaning and interpretation. The audience is introduced to this uncertainty early in the film, in the 'early rivalry' timeline: Borden, working as an assistant to another magician Milton, ties a knot around the wrists of Angier's wife Julia, who drowns during the trick because she could not get her hands free of the rope. Angier is convinced that Borden deliberately ties his preferred 'Langford double' knot instead of the slipknot that he is told to use. At his wife's funeral, an angry Angier confronts Borden and asks him which knot he tied, to which Borden answers: 'I keep asking myself that .... I just don't know.' Borden's answer, almost identical to the words that Dormer uses to reply to Burr's question as to whether he meant to shoot

Eckhart, establishes a continuity between *Insomnia* and *The Prestige*. Whereas for Dormer uncertainty is due to lack of one's knowledge of oneself, for Borden (as the first-time viewer will only understand at the end of the film) the problem is compounded by the fact that the twins are essentially two selves in one life, with all the complications of knowledge, motivation, desire and will that this creates.

The fact that 'Alfred Borden' is a composite of the two twins causes uncertainty and confusion in other characters: Cutter suspects that Borden uses 'a double' in his trick but does not realize that there are twins, and Angier refuses to believe that a double is used and becomes obsessed with discovering Borden's supposed deeper secret. Sarah and Olivia live lives of profound uncertainty, alternating between the twins without realizing it. Sarah takes to asking her 'husband' to say 'I love you' repeatedly, convinced that he means it on some days but not on others, not realizing that it is because her husband is a different man altogether on some days. Eventually the intolerable differences in behaviour and personality in 'her husband' affect her to the point that she commits suicide, while Olivia for her part walks out on Borden when he seems unaffected by Sarah's death ('It's inhuman to be so cold'), not realizing that she is (perhaps) talking to the twin who was not in love with Sarah.

Since the truth about the twins is concealed until the end of the film, it is not only the characters, but also the viewers, who are confused and made uncertain by these events. Thus when a hysterical Sarah confronts 'her husband' just before her suicide, shouting 'I know what you really are! I can't live like this,' the viewer is led to believe that this refers to Borden's erratic behaviour and adultery, but in the final analysis does not know whether Sarah in fact had guessed the truth about the twins and is referring to this instead. Likewise, Angier's reading of Borden's notebook seems to offer a confession of the 'truth' of Julia's death, with Borden writing 'I have fought with myself over that night, one half of me swearing blind that I tied a simple slip knot, and the other half convinced that I tied the Langford double.' It is only at the end of the film that we realize that this seeming confession of an individual's uncertainty and anguish is actually the truth about the Bordens being twins.

Nolan's narrative style, as in earlier films, again creates an atmosphere of uncertainty. *The Prestige* introduces a trope which, following the title of a well-known Edgar Allan Poe short story, we might call the trope of the 'purloined letter'. Here and in many later films, Nolan uses the device of a document – letter, message, pages from a book – which proves to be unreliable, with major consequences for characters' actions. In Poe's story, a scheming politician, 'Minister D—', hides in plain sight a letter stolen from a lady in the court and which threatens to embarrass her. The detective Dupin discovers the letter when the police are unable to, because he recognizes that the letter 'had been turned … inside out, redirected and resealed', and left in plain sight (Poe 1993: 146). Rather than simply stealing the letter back, Dupin also leaves a copy of it, allowing Minister D— to continue thinking he has power over the lady, thus engineering the Minister's ultimate 'political destruction' (Poe 1993: 146). Poe's famous story generated a considerable amount of discussion among psychoanalytic and post-structuralist theorists (Muller and Richardson 1988), and Nolan would doubtless have encountered it in university. The story is multilayered, an emblem not only of the unreliable missive (which is both concealed but also in plain sight), but also of the way in which the text can turn against its original intention, no longer a weapon against the lady but now (and unbeknownst to him) against Minister D—.

The trope of the 'purloined letter' is thus an apt way to describe the way in which, in Nolan's films, texts are pushed to the fore, yet may also be turned inside out, to hide omissions and deceptions, including self-deceptions. An earlier version of this is seen in *Memento*, where (according to Teddy) Leonard has removed several pages of the police dossier on his wife's murder so as to create for himself 'a puzzle you can't solve' and gives himself annotations which may not be truthful or helpful. Several versions of this trope take place in *The Prestige*. Borden's notebook which Angier reads, ostensibly stolen by Olivia at Angier's instigation (but really part of Borden's scheme), is literally a purloined document, which leads Angier on his mad quest to Tesla in Colorado. Borden's notebook is locked with a cypher using a five-letter keyword ('TESLA'), which he surrenders to Angier in order to get Fallon back. Angier refuses to believe that this is merely the keyword to the notebook and believes instead that Tesla had built a machine which Borden uses in his act. It is only when he reads Borden addressing him in Borden's notebook ('Yes, you Angier') that he realizes that Borden had deliberately allowed his notebook to fall into Angier's hands, thus using it (and Sarah) as a means of deceiving Angier and sending him on his obsessive quest. Angier later plays the same trick on Borden, after Angier is presumed to be dead, when the lawyer Owens gives Borden Angier's diary as a sign of good faith from 'Lord Caldwell'. It is through Angier's diary that Borden reads about (and the audience sees) what happens with Angier in Colorado, but again we realize the treacherous nature of the written word when

Borden reads, 'Yes, you Borden, sitting there in your cell, reading my diary, awaiting your death for my murder.'

The Prestige raises questions about texts and their complicated relations with those who write, read and possess them. Both Borden and Angier believe that they hold the key to unravelling a secret truth when they obtain the other's personal writings. Angier instigates Olivia to steal Borden's notebook believing that the supposed secret of Borden's transported man – not the double that Cutter insists is the technique – is contained within. Borden's leverage in obtaining Angier's diary is that 'Lord Caldwell' (supposedly a rich collector of magical memorabilia) wants to buy Borden's magic notes, including (once again) the technique of the transported man. Borden for his part believes that the diary will reveal the truth of Angier's death and possibly exculpate him and save him from hanging. Both men receive a shock when they discover, in the process of reading, that the writings are deliberately meant to deceive even as they explain and recount.

Nolan's 'purloined letter' motif suggests that textual meaning is hardly objective but instead is partly a function of the self who reads and who projects his or her desires and needs onto the text. This is a motif that is already suggested in *Following* (in the Young Man's reading of Cobb and the Blonde) and *Memento* (in Leonard's doctoring of the police file and his Polaroid notes to fit his revenge narrative). *The Prestige* reinforces this motif by linking purloined and deceitful texts with obsessive desires. The obsessive personal rivalry between Angier and Borden is intensified by emotions of loss, jealousy and anger, beginning with Angier's loss of Julia and his anger that Borden cannot give a satisfactory answer about the knot he uses. Later when he sees Borden with Sarah and his daughter Jess, Angier's voiceover says, 'I saw happiness, happiness that should have been mine.' Although the Borden twins seem less driven by envy of Angier than vice versa, their obsession takes a different form: when one twin is maimed after Angier sabotages their 'bullet catch' trick, the other twin deliberately maims his own hand so that their resemblance to each other is again perfect. Although the two magicians are the main instantiations, other characters also show the power of obsession: early in their careers Borden and Angier watch the magician Chung Ling Soo do the 'goldfish bowl trick', and Borden is convinced that Chung is only able to do the trick because of his shuffling crippled gait – a false gait that, in what Borden calls the 'art of self-sacrifice', Chung has to put on throughout his entire life. Sarah is initially willing to put up with having half a husband and knowing (for whatever reason) that there are days he does not truly love her, for the sake of the time that they have on the days when he does. Olivia for love of Angier is prepared to be his mole in Borden's team, and subsequently for love of Borden is prepared to betray Angier.

Obsession changes the self, rendering it unreliable (and unreadable) and justifying otherwise bizarre and unjustifiable actions. As in *Insomnia*, *The Prestige* depicts this Nolan insight through the use of the double – or in this case, sets of doubles. Angier and Borden double each other in the obsessive and imitative way that characterizes the Dormer-Finch relationship in *Insomnia*. However, the Borden twins themselves form a doubling relationship of a sort. While the Angier-Borden and Dormer-Finch pairings are typical gothic doubles in that they show the underlying dark similarities and commonalities beneath the apparent differences and dislikes, the Borden twins highlight another aspect of the double: the indistinct boundaries of the self, inasmuch as it is not possible to speak of either twin as distinctly 'Borden' or 'Fallon' but must see them as effectively interchangeable. Even if they cannot fully mimic the love for the other's loved one, the very fact that they perpetuate this strange *menage* (and would have continued it, if not for Sarah's suicide and Olivia's departure) suggests the extent to which the unique notion of the self is problematized. Angier, too, embodies this fluidity of the self: although he initially insists to Julia that his adoption of the Angier persona is merely 'changing my name', Julia insists, 'You are pretending to be someone else ... it's not just your name, it's who you are and where you're from.' Angier literalizes this when he reverts to his 'Lord Caldwell' aristocratic identity yet carries 'Angier's' obsession and anger with him, continuing to persecute Borden and attempting to wrest his magical techniques from him by using his own wealth and privilege to offer Borden the chance to give his daughter Jess a decent life after his execution.

However, the biggest and most egregious trope of the double in *The Prestige* must be the effect of the Tesla machine, which creates an exact duplicate each time it is used. The film leaves the audience pondering the question: which Angier is killed each time he performs the transported man, the original or the duplicate? Nolan uses his familiar trope of the descent to depict Angier's obsession with his act, but also to signal that this is a psychological descent where the assumed boundaries of the conventional self no longer apply. Since it is the 'prior' Angier (the one who first appears on the stage, or the 'pledge' to use Cutter's magician's terminology) who falls through the stage trap and into the water tank, this suggests that Angier kills himself and a new 'Angier' is transported to the balcony (as the

FIGURE 5 *Angier confronts his double, after performing his 'transported man' trick for the first time. The Prestige (2006), directed and screenplay by Christopher Nolan. USA: Touchstone Pictures, Warner Brothers, Newmarket Productions, Syncopy.*

'prestige'). However, the dying Angier declares to Borden that his act takes courage since Angier never knows 'if I'd be the man in the box or the prestige'. Tesla's duplicating machine works so precisely that it is impossible to tell – even for 'Angier' – which is the original and which the duplicate.

Angier, it is suggested, is particularly easy to replicate because he is a hollow man, eaten up by bitterness and envy and reduced to the one-dimensional desire to punish Borden. This point is made mockingly by the actor Gerald Root (played by Hugh Jackman, who also plays Angier/Caldwell), whom Cutter employs to be Angier's double: pulling himself out of his drunken stupor to execute his role with a *panache* that appears even to astonish Angier himself, Root says, 'Did you think you were unique Mr Angier?' Even when Angier resumes his identity as Lord Caldlow, he cannot resist visiting Borden in prison, gloating over his success in framing Borden for his murder and taunting him with the knowledge that Jess will spend the rest of her life in the care of her father's tormentor. The surviving Angier, in a sense, cannot know whether he is the magician or the aristocrat, the pledge or the prestige, because either one is defined merely by the single-minded desire for revenge, with no other depth or complexity of personality or memory to distinguish original from copy.

Again, as in Nolan's earlier films, 'inception' is practised by characters on each other to show the suggestibility of the self, its resemblance to the Other and susceptibility to the Other's influences. The Bordens' sacrifice of their personal lives to their act is inspired by the (perceived) devotion of Chung Ling Soo. The competitive careers of Borden and Angier are marked by their susceptibility to suggestions by the other person, as they seek to outdo each other. Thus Angier goes on his quest to find Tesla because Borden plants the idea in his head, by deliberately allowing Angier to see him at the exposition looking at Tesla's machine, by having a fake electrical apparatus onstage during his act and by making 'TESLA' the key to the cipher protecting his notebook (which he allows Angier to acquire). Borden for his part succumbs to the temptation to visit Angier's act (despite being warned not to do so by his twin), which is precisely what Angier intends and which enables him to frame Borden for the murder. The suggestibility of the self is also seen in other characters: Angier sends Olivia over to Borden to spy on him, but by suggesting that she pretend to betray Angier, he seems to actually plant that idea into her, and she ends up really betraying him and falling in love with one of the twins.

Nolan's use of the doppelganger motif in *The Prestige* develops the view suggested in earlier films, that the self is fundamentally porous to a variety of influences, that it practises self-deception in order to fulfil its own desires, and that professional pride easily slips into an obsession that renders the self unrecognizable. In *The Prestige*, neither of the competing magicians can be said to triumph at the end, and neither finds the fulfilling personal life that they both profess to seek. Borden is reunited with his daughter but loses both his wife and his brother (and in the latter, arguably loses half his identity and personality). Angier succeeds in the sense that he fulfils his malicious plan to destroy 'Borden' but fails in that he does not count on there being a surviving twin. While Angier seems to have lost more (his wife Julia, his lover Olivia, a whole series of murdered doubles, and finally his own life too), in the final analysis Borden's murder of Angier is as ruthless as Angier's own actions and brings both men down to the same moral level.

As Nietzsche famously says, 'Whoever fights with monsters should see to it that he does not become one himself. And when you stare for a long time into an abyss, the abyss stares back into you' (2002: 69). For Nietzsche, 'Man is something that should be overcome,' and to merely obey the inherited values of 'culture' or 'the state' in an unquestioning manner was 'weakness' and evil (1961: 41–5, 75–7). Yet the abandonment of society's inherited values necessitated replacing them with a 'new creation,' 'a new beginning' forged by the 'will to power' of the 'superman' (1961: 55; 1968: 115). Nolan's Nietzschean exploration of the hollowness of the self comprehends no great vision to replace it. The obsessive drives of Borden and Angier push them beyond the actions and achievements of ordinary men, but in the end they find no lasting truths, only their own monstrous hollowness reflected back on them – a condition literalized by the trope of the doppelganger. As Webber (1996: 6) notes, 'Doppelgänger stories are also rife in the effects of mise-en-abyme, whereby figures or structures are reflected within each other .... The mise-en-abyme of emblematic figures at once serves to repeat and so affirm ad infinitum the identity for which they stand, and yet to cast the sign of identity into abysmal or groundless nonentity.' Nolan's narrative structure reinforces the abysmal emptiness of the human condition, the infinite regression in which (at one point in the film) the story is told in the form of Borden reading Angier's diary, which tells of Angier reading Borden's notebook, during which narration the action unfolds before the audience. This reminder that meaning (including the meaning of human existence) is no transcendent truth, but a tale within a tale (within a tale), is developed in Nolan's subsequent allegories of space/time and the self.

3

Science fiction, indeterminate selves and moral action: *Inception* and *Interstellar*

Nolan's science fiction films: Space, time and the self

The Batman trilogy, Nolan's major commitment to the big-budget blockbuster movie system, in a sense interrupts the films in which he develops his signature themes and storytelling style. Just as *Batman Begins* (2005) intervenes between *Insomnia* and *The Prestige*, so likewise did *The Dark Knight* (2008) intervene between *The Prestige* and *Inception*, and *The Dark Knight Rises* (2012) intervene between *Inception* and *Interstellar*. This is not to say that there are no thematic or stylistic continuities whatsoever between the Batman trilogy and the other Nolan films, but that the premises of the DC Comics universe imposed a unity on the trilogy that did not completely allow

Nolan the freedom to fully develop some of the issues raised in the earlier films. Seen analytically rather than in chronological sequence, it is clear that *Inception* and *Interstellar* form a stronger filmic link with each other (and in some ways with earlier films) than with any of the Batman trilogy, and vice versa. Both films are explorations of space and time, one through the premise of the dream state, the other through quantum astrophysics. Both films use space-time to elaborate on the theory of the self: its instabilities due to lack of self-knowledge, its susceptibility to (self-)deception, obsession, and external influences, and the moral problems that arise when one has to act in conditions of limited knowledge and constrained social resources.

Inception (2010) is very likely the Nolan film that has received the most critical attention over the years. This is perhaps because it is a film which has all the elements of a Hollywood blockbuster – a spectacular cast, a fast-paced plot and slick action sequences – and combines these with many of Nolan's signature filmic devices such as non-sequential storytelling, ambiguity of meaning (at both the thematic and structural levels), the theme of the divided self, and the obsessive mission or aspiration. The combination of star power and the complexity of Nolan's storytelling techniques seems to have pushed *Inception* to the fore in terms of critical attention. In this sense it bears some comparison with the Matrix trilogy (1999–2003, directed by the Wachowskis), which also combined blockbuster elements with themes of technological control and illusion versus reality, and which has also gained a cult following. Unlike the Wachowskis, Nolan largely eschews CGI for his action scenes, and his narrative complexity creates more fundamental ambiguity for the viewer than the Matrix films, but there is some basis for comparison nevertheless. *Inception's* use of the dream state, in addition to allowing fantastical action sequences, also evokes many of the psychological issues (concealment, deception, symbolic manifestations, doubling) seen in the early Nolan films.

Interstellar (2014) followed fairly closely after *Inception*, with one film (the 2012 *The Dark Knight Rises* in Nolan's Batman trilogy) intervening. *Interstellar* might be seen as a pivotal film, on the one hand continuing some of the themes of knowledge and selfhood seen in earlier films, but on the other hand also developing an emergent theme seen in the Batman trilogy and later films like *Dunkirk*: the theme of social morality, of the one and the many, of social factions, and how individual needs and desires stack up against the interests of the whole of society or the human race. While *Interstellar's* premise of the worm hole (with its distortion of space and time) allows Nolan to transpose his epistemological themes into this science fiction setting, the dystopian social condition provides the setting for Nolan to develop his theme of the zero-sum game, where individuals are forced to choose between two courses of action, each with negative consequences. *Interstellar* signals Nolan's growing interest in the later stage of his career with Utilitarian moral ideas and the calculus of means and ends. These moral ideas link to his epistemological concerns in that the individual's choices are complicated by lack of full knowledge and disclosure: of the self's nature and motives, of others in society, and of the world we live in.

Inception: Dream premise, narrative complexity, and epistemic condition

One of the main critical debates has been inspired by the film's trope of the dream-within-dream (within dream), and the various interpretative possibilities that this trope and Nolan's mises en scène create. Tallman (2012: 19) sums up the four main interpretative possibilities: the 'most real' interpretation that most of the film takes place in waking time (except when we are explicitly told the characters are entering a dream world), and Cobb is really reunited with his children at the end; the 'mostly real' one, which differs from the first in that Cobb and Saito remain in limbo and Cobb does not really get reunited with his children; the 'mostly dream' one, where everything that happens to Cobb after he goes to sleep in Yusuf's basement is a dream; and the 'full dream' one, where all the action in the film is in a dream, into which Cobb emerges after awakening from the limbo he shared with Mal. These various interpretative possibilities have implications for our view of character and plot: as Terjesen (2012: 54) points out, 'our art relief (as opposed to genuine relief) at seeing Cobb come to terms with Mal's death will seem disingenuous if it turns out that the film is meant to end with Cobb trapped in a dream'. Not only do these interpretations affect our engagement with the film's characters, they also have implications for our own sense of reality: as Weijers (2012: 103) remarks, 'someone who has seen *Inception* should realise that they can't be sure of whether the life they are familiar with is actually a real one', since the film essentially makes the point that it is impossible while we are dreaming to be fully sure that we are in a dream.

While critics are correct to note the film's structural ambiguities which prevent any definitive answer as to the question of whether an action takes place in dreams or 'real' time-space, this ambiguity does not exempt the viewer from making a response to (and inevitably a judgement of) characters and their actions. If the dream sequences are embedded within real life (the 'most real' scenario), then dream actions certainly have consequences in the real world and must be evaluated like all real actions. If the whole film is a dream (the 'full dream' scenario), then the dream-actions are all that the audience has, the entire basis for the audience's response and interpretation, and must still be seen as meaningful and significant, if only of characters' natures and intentions. The many thematic continuities between *Inception* and Nolan's earlier films also suggest that Nolan in this film is continuing his exploration of notions of the self, its motivations and influences, the forms of knowledge on which the self bases its actions, and the morality of those actions. Nolan's narrative complexities, and the epistemic complications posed by the different dream levels, do not negate moral responses. Rather, as with all Nolan films, epistemic complications are an inherent component of the experiences of the self, of the conditions under which individuals have to exist and function. Dreams can thus be a test bed for the self's epistemic functions, moral choices, actions and consequences.

The protagonist, Cobb – a name Nolan recycles from the enigmatic criminal in *Following* – is like many Nolan protagonists a figure who operates on the edge of legality, as a dream-raider who digs out corporate secrets (and also commits what is essentially corporate sabotage) for his clients. He is also struggling with the guilt of his wife's death and his role in it, and with the desire to be reunited with his children. He and his crew are extremely ruthless in the course of carrying out their jobs, killing anyone who gets in their way, and using whatever form of deception is necessary. In Cobb's defence it could be argued that the people he kills are all in the dreamworld and that the ends (being reunited with his children and stopping Fischer's conglomerate from becoming a monopolizing superpower) justify the means. This does not change the fact that Cobb in his customary dream-mode of operation is an individual well versed in violence and deception, his moral slipperiness a corollary to other Nolan characters like the Young Man and Cobb in *Following*, Leonard and Teddy in *Memento*, Dormer and Finch in *Insomnia*, and Angier and Borden in *The Prestige*.

Cobb does not have an obvious double the way Dormer has in Finch, or Borden in Angier, but in a sense all the characters in *Inception* can be said to mirror or echo his unconscious qualities, since for most of the film they exist as characters in dreams that they share with Cobb. The closest reflection of Cobb's inner state is probably Mal, whom we are told is a projection of Cobb's psyche, which takes the form of his dead wife. Since her character is dead in real life, she has arguably less of an independent personality than the other main characters, her personality dependent on Cobb's memories and projections. If her name derives from the French – plausible, given both Nolan's penchant for plays on names, and Mal's French origins – then she represents the 'sick' or dark aspects of Cobb's personality that he perhaps refuses to acknowledge (Winchur 2012: 45). Apart from Mal, other characters like Eames, Arthur, Saito, Yusuf and Ariadne also echo and reveal aspects of Cobb's personality.

Nolan's narrative complexity in *Inception* develops the fabulist mise en abyme that he creates in *The Prestige*, with Borden reading Angier's diary (in which Angier is recording the events that the audience sees, including at one point Angier reading Borden's notebook). Bernard (2017: 233–34) posits that the films' 'postmodernist self-reflexiveness' consists (among other things) in a mode of storytelling that leaves audiences 'suspended between … reality and fiction, between surface and depth'. If so, Nolan certainly signals to the audience the self-reflexive viewing that is required: in a scene during Ariadne's audition to join Cobb's crew, she literally creates a mise en abyme in the dream city by turning two mirrors to face each other to create an infinite regression of images.

FIGURE 6 *Ariadne creates a mise en abyme by causing parts of her constructed dream landscape to become mirrors of each other. Inception (2010), directed and written by Christopher Nolan. USA: Warner Brothers, Legendary Entertainment, Syncopy.*

In this fashion, audiences are forewarned of the narrative infoldings and regressions that abound in this film. The opening sequence of *Inception* is deliberately confusing and compressed: there is a segment which (by the end of the film) we recognize to be Cobb descending down to Limbo to fetch Saito, who has become an old man in the accelerated dream-time of Limbo (what we might call sub-scene 1a). However, this abruptly segues to an encounter between Cobb and a younger Saito, with Cobb trying to break into Saito's safe to steal an envelope (sub-scene 1b). Continuity between 1a and 1b is suggested by the architecture of Saito's mansion and the presence of his bodyguards in dark suits. This scene also turns out to be a dream, when the film jump-cuts to an explosion and reveals Cobb and his team with Saito in his 'love nest' (sub-scene 1c). This setting is in turn revealed to be a dream, when the film jump-cuts to Cobb and his team on a high-speed train in Japan, where they have shared a dream with Saito in an attempt to steal secrets from his mind (sub-scene 1d). At this point the viewer is prepared to see the whole opening sequence as an action arc embedded in different levels of dreams. However, by the end of the film we realize that while this may describe sub-scenes 1b–1d, 1a is actually much later in the history of events, in the late stage of the campaign to plant an idea in Fischer's mind, and seems to have no connection with the other three sub-scenes which occur before Cobb starts working for Saito.

Subsequent scenes appear to tell a more-or-less linear story: Saito recruiting Cobb and team for a job of inception on Fischer, the team's preparations, the Fischer job and its complications which push the team into deeper and deeper dream levels, the successful completion of the job, the team waking up on the plane, and finally

Cobb's reunion with his children. However, embedded even within the chronological sequences are achronological scenes, in which we are told the backstory of Cobb and Mal, and see them in Limbo and in the hotel room from which Mal jumps. The sequential segment also moves into different dream levels, the deeper levels embedded within the higher dreams: the rainy urban setting where the team kidnaps Fischer and where Saito is wounded (dream level I); the hotel where Cobb as 'Mr Charles' poses as Fischer's dream-security man to gain his confidence (level II); the snow landscape where the team assists Fischer in breaking into his father's safe and where Mal suddenly appears and shoots Fischer (level III); and Limbo (level IV) where Cobb and Ariadne go to retrieve Fischer (who drops down there when Mal kills him) and also Saito (who by this time has died from his injuries in the higher levels).

If the reverse narrative in *Memento* confuses the viewer's sense of cause and effect, and consequently fosters a suspension of moral judgement, the embedded narrative structure of *Inception* ruptures the sense of a coherent universe of action, blurring the reality and consequentiality of action by shifting the action from one dream level to another (during which sequentiality also has to be disrupted or suspended at times). In place of the rules of time and space that we are accustomed to, *Inception* imposes a more fluid and unpredictable set of scenarios, whose rules have to be explained by characters (who themselves do not always seem to be sure). Thus near the beginning of the film (sub-scene 1b), Cobb kills the wounded Arthur in the knowledge that dying in the dream world will wake Arthur up in the real. Later in the rainy urban dream (level I), Eames wants to kill the wounded Saito to wake him up, but now it is explained by Yusuf that they are too heavily sedated (using Yusuf's special compound), and dying in this state will not wake them up but drop them into Limbo, which is 'unconstructed dream space', 'raw infinite unconscious'. Near the end of the film, when Cobb rescues the old Saito from Limbo, it is suggested that Saito (seen reaching for Cobb's gun) kills himself so that he and Cobb can return to wakefulness, which seems to contradict Yusuf's explanation to Eames.

Another ambiguity concerns whose unconscious is featured in each segment. The Fischer job is meant to be a venture into Fischer's unconscious (while he dreams on the Sydney-to-LA flight), but in the hotel (level II), Ariadne confronts Cobb with the realization that as they go deeper into Fischer's unconscious, they are somehow also going deeper into Cobb's. Ariadne's claim seems to be substantiated by the fact that, although the action in levels I to III certainly seems to centre on Fischer (his relationship with Browning and his father, his desire to penetrate into his father's safe and the secret it contains), it is also populated by elements of Cobb's unconscious: the train which crashes into Cobb's car in level I (evoking the train which kills Mal and Cobb in their Limbo time), the appearance of his children running in the hotel lobby in level II, and the appearance of Mal at critical scenes throughout.

In level I, the wounded Saito promises Cobb that he will honour the arrangement (to clear Cobb's name and allow him to go back to the United States), but Cobb explains to him that if Saito dies and drops into Limbo, he will not even remember the arrangement: 'You're going to be lost down there so long that you're going to become an old man.' Yet when Saito does drop into Limbo and become an old man there, after he wakes up on the plane, he clearly can remember the arrangement, and takes out his phone to make the call that will clear Cobb through immigration. By far the most confusing information offered to the audience is the concept of the 'totem', which is meant to be a unique object that will tell its owner whether he or she is dreaming or awake. Arthur shows Ariadne his totem, a red die, and tells her that only he knows the unique feel, 'the balance and weight of this particular die'. This is why Ariadne later customizes her own totem (a chess piece) and refuses to let Arthur touch it. Yet Cobb's totem which he constantly handles – a metal top – is later revealed to belong to Mal originally. When Cobb recounts to Ariadne and Mal how he succeeded in persuading Mal to wake up from their Limbo-time together, the audience sees Cobb spinning the top and placing it in a safe; the implication is that he succeeds in manipulating Mal because he has access to her supposedly individual totem and because he can move it at will in her mind. In the opening sequence (sub-scene 1a) when Cobb in Limbo is brought before the old Saito, Cobb's gun and totem are placed on the table before Saito, and he handles and spins Cobb's totem, saying that he knows what it is. It may be that Saito can handle Cobb's totem because this is a Limbo-totem rather than the object in the real world, but this does not explain Saito's uncanny recognition of what is meant to be Cobb's unique totem, which in turn (we are later told) was Mal's totem. This confusion about the unique and yet not-unique quality of the totem no doubt contributes to the ambiguity of the final scene that has intrigued many viewers, when Cobb is reunited with his children and the film ends with the top spinning on the table.

Dream-selves, 'inception' and morality

Narrative structure, mise en scène and symbolism thus combine to create structural ambiguities which are not easily resolved – which, in fact, may lead to endless inconclusive debate. Both Nolan and actor Michael Caine (who plays Professor Miles) have said that they have a conclusive answer to the film's riddles, particularly which scenes are real and which are in dreams. Commenting on *Inception* in an interview, Nolan says:

> I've always believed that if you make a film with ambiguity, it needs to be based on a sincere interpretation. If it's not, then it will contradict itself, or it will be somehow insubstantial and end up making the audience feel cheated. I think the only way to make ambiguity satisfying is to base it on a very solid point of view of what you think is going on, and then allow the ambiguity to come from the inability of the character to know, and the alignment of the audience with that character.
>
> (Capps 2010)

Caine reveals that when he queried Nolan about which scenes were real and which were not, he was told '"Well, when you're in the scene, it's reality." So get that – if I'm in it, it's reality. If I'm not in it, it's a dream' (Newbould 2018). Caine's comment seems to reinforce the 'most real' reading of the film (Tallman 2012: 19), that Cobb actually wakes up on the plane and is really reunited with his children at the end. However, although Nolan's comment is compatible with Caine's, Nolan does not actually come out and agree with the 'most real' reading (that Cobb is awake at the end of the film). Moreover, we need as always to beware the 'intentional fallacy' of maintaining that the director's view is the definitive interpretation of the work. Even if the 'most real' interpretation were the best option, this does not entirely remove the ambiguous and open-ended quality of the film. We are still left with questions such as who is dreaming in each dream level (and what role does this leave the others in the dream); what is the role (if any) of totems and how do they comment on the film's action; what is the morality of action committed in a dream, and what does such action reveal (if anything) about characters' personalities and desires; and what is the relationship between dreams and each character's reality.

These and other of the film's questions and ambiguities might be summed up (at the risk of simplifying somewhat) in the overarching question: what does the act of 'inception' signify? That is to say: if it is possible for some other person or influence to clearly and distinctly plant an idea into our minds, then what does this say about individuality and free will? If inception is not truly an external force, then to what extent does one collaborate or be complicit with the inception, and to what purpose – why does the self accept the inception? What is the relationship between the dream-self and the waking one, and what consequences (if any) do dream actions have for the self?

Dreams are the expression of unconscious desires and hidden aspects of the self, perhaps more evidently than even the unreliable memory of Leonard Shelby, the insomnia-enhanced stresses of Dormer, or the obsessive ambitions of Borden and Angier. The trope of physical descent in earlier films – Dormer diving through trap doors to enter into the morally murky world of Finch, Angier dropping through stage traps to perfect his transported man act and in the process kill one of his own selves – finds its corollary in *Inception*'s trope of dropping off to sleep, and in sleep descending from one dream state into a deeper one. If we see the descent into deeper and deeper dream levels as the exploration of hidden depths of the self, then this answers one of the film's puzzles: the descent into Fischer's unconscious is in fact also a descent into Cobb's, because these two (out of all the characters in the film) have the most unresolved inner conflicts, and thus their neuroses dominate any dream level in which they are both found. This view suggests that Professor Miles (who is never seen dreaming in the film) is the most psychologically balanced or healthy character, while Arthur (whom Eames accuses of being 'unimaginative' and who flatly tells Cobb that 'Mal is dead') is too pragmatic to let any inner conflict affect his work. Eames and Ariadne fall somewhere in the middle, the former's essentially amoral hollowness allowing him to adopt different disguises (including one transsexual manifestation as a blonde woman, perhaps an allusion to the Blonde femme fatale in *Following*), the latter's obsession with Cobb's problems perhaps indicating some emotional entanglement with him, including possibly an unconfessed erotic one – this may be symbolized by Ariadne shooting Mal in Limbo near the end of the film, thus ridding Cobb of his old love interest which is also her competition.

On the surface the film might be seen as a dramatization of the quest for psychological and emotional closure: for Fischer, the resolution of his estrangement from a looming but absent father, and for Cobb, the resolution of his feelings of guilt over his wife's death. Fischer appears to penetrate to the heart of his relationship with his father (represented by the safe beside the sick bed) and discovers that his father has kept the pinwheel from Fischer's childhood and that his father was 'disappointed' not that Fischer did not measure up to him, but that he would try to do nothing more than follow in his father's footsteps. Fischer's emotional-psychological journey appears to end with the resolution that he will strive to be his 'own man'. Cobb confronts his projection of Mal and confesses that she had come to question the reality of her waking world (which in turn led to her suicide) because Cobb had planted that idea in her, in an attempt to get her to leave Limbo. He also tells her that he did fulfil his promise that they would 'grow old together' (as the audience sees an old couple walking together in the Limbo world) and that since they had their 'time together', he concludes, 'I have to let you go.'

The concept of inception throws a spanner in the works of these apparent psychical resolutions. As we have seen, suggestibility – and the moral and identity questions associated with it – is at the heart of Nolan's oeuvre. Fischer's desire to be his 'own man' is highly ironic, given that this was the goal for which Saito commissioned Cobb. The mise en scène of the moments that lead to Fischer's resolution heightens the irony: in level III he opens his dying father's vault using a combination (528491) that was planted in his mind on level II when the Blonde (really Eames in disguise) gives him her strange six-digit phone number. The number is also a combination of the numbers of the two rooms (528 and 491) that the crew use in the hotel in level II. Although it is Fischer who randomly shouts out this number in Level I, when threatened by Cobb's crew, the combination does not work until it is reinforced in his mind by the crew's actions. Fischer announces his resolution to be his 'own man' after these different psychological levers have been used on him, as he is sitting by the river (in level I), confiding in the avuncular figure of Browning who is actually Eames in disguise. All these plot elements make his declaration of independence to be heavily ironic.

Cobb's psychic resolution is even more fraught and impure than Fischer's. In Cobb's final confrontation with Mal (in level IV), after confessing to his role in Mal's mental illness and suicide, Cobb tells Ariadne that he knows he cannot stay with Mal anymore because 'she doesn't exist'. This is supposed to mark his healing and psychological reintegration – the act of forgiving himself that Ariadne tells him is required – after which he is able to complete the Fischer job and be reunited with his children (Winchur 2012: 44). However, Mal is more often seen as a random force of violence than as the loved one with whose loss Cobb has to come to terms. Her hostility to others in the film is gratuitous and inexplicable: she shoots Arthur in the leg (opening sub-scene 1b), stabs Ariadne during her dream-orientation as Cobb is trying to recruit her, tries to stab Ariadne with a broken glass when the latter sneaks into Cobb's dream in Paris, and shoots Fischer in level III. Mal's slick and professional acts of violence resemble the 'militarized' armed men that protect Fischer (in levels I to III) and Saito (in opening sub-sequence 1b), or Cobb himself and his crew. The image of Cobb's lost wife has somehow become tainted by elements of the violent and militarized world in which Cobb and other corporate operatives move.

This suggestion that Mal is more of a free radical absorbing the violence and chaos of Cobb's profession, than an embodiment of his memories of and feelings about his dead wife, is reinforced by the other examples of sharing of phrases, scenes and totems between different personas. When Saito confronts Cobb on the rooftop after the failure of the Saito job, he tries to recruit Cobb for the inception project on Fischer, promising that the reward will be Cobb's clearance to return to the United States: 'Do you want to take a leap of faith … ?' When Cobb tells his backstory to Ariadne (in level I), and the audience sees Mal standing on the ledge of the Paris hotel, Mal tries to get Cobb to jump with her (believing that this will wake them both up) by saying 'I'm asking you to take a leap of faith.' Cobb in turn uses the same phrase near the end of the film, when he tries to persuade the old Saito to kill himself in Limbo so that he can be 'kicked' up to the waking realm. A similar sharing or overlap of provenances is seen in the spinning top, which over the course of the film has been seen or accounted for as belonging to both Mal and Cobb and handled by both Cobb and Saito. The film deliberately undercuts the notion of uniqueness of expressions, totems, character traits, in order to show the suggestibility and porousness of identity. If Cobb and crew are seen to be successful in incepting an idea in Fischer, this is only because the film as a whole shows inception to be ubiquitous and systemic.

The disturbingly ubiquitous nature of shared dream-action, catchphrases, totems and other elements raises the question of self-deception or one's complicity in inception. As we have seen in earlier Nolan films, Nolan places his protagonists in situations where they become willingly complicit in their own moral decline. The revelation in *Memento* that Teddy uses Leonard to kill for Teddy's profit is not as shocking as the realization that Leonard (in his brief moments of clarity before his memory fades) lies to himself through his notes and tattoos so that he can continue the quest for 'vengeance' that has become his raison d'être. Cobb's condition, within the multiple layers of dreams he experiences, is simply that of Leonard taken to its logical conclusion: 'It's one thing to lie to oneself; it's another to not even know whether one is lying to oneself or not' (Fischer 2011: 38). In *The Prestige*, the trickery and manipulation practised by Borden and Angier on each other, in many ways pales beside what they do to themselves (graphically depicted in how the Borden twins amputate the healthy twin's fingers, and the look of horror and panic on the face of the 'Angier' who is shot by 'himself' at the first trial of the Tesla machine). In a real sense, Angier and Borden are so successful in baiting and manipulating each other because each is psychologically and obsessively tied to the other. *Inception* continues this theme, the confused blurring of dream-elements from different personalities suggesting the ease with which the protagonists participate in the internalization of traits and influences of others.

In *Inception*, Fischer contributes to his own inception because of his need for closure with and approval from his father. Fischer supplies the seeds for Cobb's crew to manipulate his mind, not just in supplying the 'random' combination 528491 which ultimately coalesces into the combination to his father's safe in level III. Fischer also becomes more and more an active participant in the action, the deeper they go (and the closer towards the confrontation between father and son): from bewildered kidnap victim in level I, to initially suspicious but increasing trusting in level II, to an active fighter and agent alongside Cobb's crew in level III. The transition from levels II to III is particularly marked: although Cobb at the end of the level II sequence tells Fischer that they are going to go into Browning's unconscious to find out his supposed motivation for betraying Fischer, it is increasingly obvious in level III that they are not in Browning's unconscious (Browning does not even appear in this sequence), particularly when they break into Maurice Fischer's room, which is clearly a scene from Fischer's own psyche. As Eames stresses when they initially strategize for the Fischer job, the key to their success is Fischer's 'relationship with the father': Fischer is a willing accomplice because he does want a positive resolution, one that affirms his father's love and approval for him (despite the fact that his father is already dead, as he well knows).

Malloy (2012: 133) observes that 'in *Inception*, the protagonists are granted redemption, of a sort, not because they are caught or because of the moral decreptitude of their victim – we really don't learn enough about Robert Fischer to judge him – but because of the supposed benefit their crime will bring the victim'. Invoking Plato's argument for censorship on moral grounds, Malloy (2012: 133) maintains that 'in Plato's eyes, though, that wouldn't be enough', since viewers might be induced to imitate characters' actions believing that they are morally justified. The same caveat would hold in *Inception*, and Nolan's self-reflexive elements are there to warn audiences against a simple acceptance of characters' justifications, motives and actions.

Corporations, ideology and capitalism's hollow man

Cobb, the protagonist of this film, exhibits the greatest degree of (self-)inception and complicity. Cobb's overarching desire is to return to the US and be reunited with his children, and it is easy to be caught up in Cobb's cause and in the nail-biting excitement of his struggle to accomplish it. However, this would blind us to the fact that Cobb's actions are generally tainted by his association with dubious parties and his use of questionable methods. Cobb is essentially a thief, as the opening sequence shows: he is employed by a group called Cobol Engineering to steal corporate secrets from Saito's mind. The name of this corporation may be significant: a 'cobold' or 'kobold' (in its alternate spelling) is a spirit in Germanic folklore, and Nietzsche in *Beyond Good and Evil* uses the term to demonize the 'imperious' human impulse to install systems of knowledge, and even 'mistaken knowledge,' as philosophical truth (Nietzsche 2002: 9). Nietzsche's demonization of the invisible act of implanting 'mistaken knowledge' into man's minds could easily apply to the concept of 'inception', except that the influence of market ideology is even more insidious in that it is not the work of a single identifiable agent like Cobb, but pervasive and invisible.

Throughout the course of the film Cobb is under the power and influence of corporate values and goals. Winchur (2012: 47) goes so far as to say that 'the film works as corporate propaganda', disguising 'white-collar violence' in the 'benign setting of private turmoil'. Cobb's decision to take on the work for Cobol, despite knowing what kind of organization it is, reveals his affinity with them, and (given Nolan's attention to names) it is perhaps no accident that 'Cobb' sounds almost like a derivative from or diminutive of 'Cobol'. This job also lacks the moral justification of the Fischer job: Cobb works for Cobol for payment, not for the promise of being reunited with his children that Saito later offers him.

The later Fischer job initially seems like a reversal of the Saito one, almost like an opportunity for redemption by taking on a morally sanctioned job: not stealing something, but implanting or conferring something; not against Saito, but for him; the client (Saito) as companion and friend, not as faceless and ruthless corporation (Cobol). Yet this distinction is a highly dubious one: apart from the countless deceptions and acts of violence that are perpetrated on Fischer, it is not clear that Saito is any better than Cobol. While there is a suggestion of camaraderie in Cobb rescuing him in Limbo, the utility of that action is obvious, since without Saito conscious and mentally sound back on the plane, there would be no phone call to clear Cobb's re-entry to the United States. Saito justifies the Fischer job as preventing the latter's corporation from becoming a 'new superpower', but the film shows no evidence of this. Saito's competitive motives and his own vast power – he effectively sabotages Fischer's private jet, casually buys an airline just to ensure that Cobb's crew has complete control over the first-class cabin where Fischer is seated and has the power to influence the actions of the US Immigration and Customs Enforcement – are perhaps even more sinister than Cobol's violent but ineffectual sanctions against Cobb and his team.

If the two corporations that Cobb works for are morally questionable, so too is the company that Cobb keeps, the environmental influences that shape his thoughts and actions. It is significant that one of Cobb's crew in the Saito job, Nash, betrays Cobb to Saito, which allows the latter to intercept Cobb on the rooftop. Eames is not just a thief (as all the crew are, fundamentally), but also a shapeshifter (no one else in the film demonstrates this uncanny ability) who suggests qualities of Satan in John Milton's *Paradise Lost*, Loki in Norse Mythology, and other figures of supernatural mischief. Yusuf is essentially a drug peddler, the basement where people come to partake of his dream-compounds possessing all the dark torpid squalor of an opium den. In agreeing to join Cobb's team, he is simply expanding his scope as a drug dealer.

Within the value system in which Cobb finds himself, vague moral ends – to be reunited with one's children, to save the world from a supposed 'new superpower', to help someone resolve his father issues – are not sufficient to prevent moral contagion. Nolan's films suggest the dangers of being susceptible to external influences while living in a world where market values of individualism, greed and ruthlessness predominate. Cobb seeks to justify himself by separating his ends (with their veneer of morality) from means which have little or no moral justification. Yet *Inception*, like many of Nolan's films, questions ends-justification. This is seen in the trope of recklessness, which imposes selfish desire upon uncertain facts and outcomes – which, in effect, exploits uncertainty in order to argue that the course of action one desires is as good as any other. In *Inception*, this is seen in the idea of the 'leap of faith' propagated by several characters. Whether used by Saito to persuade Cobb to take on the Fischer job, or by Mal to get Cobb to jump off the hotel ledge with her, or by Cobb to get Saito to kill himself in Limbo and thus wake up back on the plane, the idea of a 'leap of faith' is a manipulative ploy thinly disguised as greater good or better goal. The audience cannot be sure, any more than the characters, that practising inception on Fischer will result in a better world order or that killing oneself will result in a better life on another level of consciousness. The dubiousness of the supposed end only highlights the immorality of the means to that end, whether it be blackmailing one's husband or invading someone else's mind. In lieu of certain or even reliable knowledge about outcomes, the 'leap of faith' is merely selfish recklessness. Cobb's actions throughout the film embody this recklessness: as Barkman (2012: 148) puts it, 'I believe Cobb *is* morally to blame, since he was negligent as to the effects of inception.' Although the full consequences of his actions were not knowable, the very fact of acting without knowledge of consequences is blatant recklessness, 'and his recklessness led to his wife throwing herself from the hotel window' (Barkman 2012: 149).

The French song that is repeated throughout the film, used by the crew as a warning that a 'kick' is about to incur – a phrase from Edith Piaf's '*Non, Je Ne Regrette Rien*' – could well serve as Cobb's *apologia*. Since Cobb seems to get what he wants at the end – a safe return to the United States and a reunion with his children – like Piaf he seems to be declaring that he regrets nothing. The spinning of the top in the final scene is not a litmus test as to whether he is finally awake or dreaming, but rather a possible signal of his insouciance, that the totem will continue to be in use because he will continue with his work of dream-espionage and dream-inception, moral questions notwithstanding. Cobb in *Inception* may thus be a more complex version of the more enigmatic Cobb in *Following*: both are functionaries, hollow men who unquestioningly serve the powerful in society. While they may give the illusion of human struggle or striving, in the final analysis they merely serve to reflect the moral problematic of their society and time.

Interstellar and dystopia: Zero-sum scenarios and moral choices

If in *Inception* characters all have to function within a ruthless world of competing powerful corporations, the dystopian premise in *Interstellar* is no less disturbing. A 'blight' on crops has meant that Earth is unable to continue sustaining its population, so that mankind's future has to be sought on other worlds. NASA is a crippled organization, its resources severely limited by the diversion of resources away from the 'wasteful' technologies (as one character puts it) that characterized the era of the Cold War. What the film presents is a crippled agrarian world, where farming is considered to be a noble profession, where education is a luxury only accessible to a privileged few, where technology is stagnant and machine parts cannibalized and recycled, and where mankind's primary focus is on survival rather than the advancement of knowledge and civilization. Nolan effectively sets up a Malthusian scenario, where population has exceeded society's capacity to provide for it (Malthus 1993). While Malthus believed that this was the inevitable result of the rate of human reproduction exceeding the rate of any agricultural increase, in *Interstellar* the premise of the blight and crop failure is the catalyst.

The film's protagonist, Cooper, is an ex-NASA pilot (let go when the agency's funding was cut) turned disgruntled farmer, a widower who ekes out a rough existence with his daughter Murphy, son Tom, and father-in-law Donald. While Tom is content to take over the family farm and struggle within the status quo, Murphy (like her father) is more intellectually curious and adventurous. The bond between father and daughter is particularly close, and the film establishes this with episodes such as Murphy stowing away in Cooper's truck when he goes off in search of the site (eventually revealed as NASA's covert base) specified in the mysterious coordinates he receives, or Cooper's hand on Murphy's on the laptop touchpad as he guides her in steering the hijacked Indian Air Force drone. The father-daughter bond is tested when Cooper is asked by his old NASA mentor Professor Brand to undertake a mission to ascertain which one of three possible inhabitable worlds – suddenly made accessible to mankind by the appearance of a wormhole – will become mankind's future home. Cooper decides to go, even though Murphy wants him to stay, and their emotional confrontation sets the tone for much of their following relationship, which spans decades of time and light years of distance.

The film is full of hard choices of the zero-sum type. Cooper has to choose between staying with his children (and very likely seeing them gradually waste away, as we later see with the illness of Tom's son and wife) and leaving them in the hope of finding a better home for them and all of mankind. Professor Brand, with NASA's constrained resources, has to choose between a 'Plan A' which involves moving mankind off the planet, or a backup 'Plan B' which involves just saving about 5,000 human embryos. Later the expeditionary crew on the 'Endurance', with limited fuel and life-sustaining resources, have to choose between the planet explored by Dr Mann and that explored by Edmunds (with the complication that Brand, the Professor's daughter, is in love with Edmunds and wishes to see him again). Professor Brand's Plan A is stalled because he cannot solve the equations that would allow them to put the whole of the human race into space, so that his secret agenda is really to push forward Plan B. Near the end of the film, with resources on the 'Endurance' depleted, Cooper has to sacrifice himself by ejecting himself in the Ranger 2 module so that Brand would have enough fuel and bioresources to reach Edmund's planet, which is their final hope.

Interstellar thus sets up a moral problem that characterizes this middle-to-later stage of Nolan's career: the problem of the interests of the individual versus those of society, the few versus the many. This was a moral problem very much to the fore in the long industrial revolution in Europe from the late eighteenth century to the twentieth, and (in addition to Malthus' gloomy projections) occupied the thoughts of thinkers like Adam Smith, Jeremy Bentham and John Stuart Mill. Smith in his seminal *Wealth of Nations* was inclined to believe that 'mutual self-interest' would ensure that things worked for the common good; in maximizing one's own best interests, one would also tend to serve the interests of society as a whole, for example when factory owners seek to offer goods of better quality and lower price so as to attract more customers or when the wealth of such producers adds to the stock of 'national wealth' (Smith 1937: 11, 14). Elsewhere (in his *Theory of Moral Sentiments*) Smith says that the 'utility' of man's social ties – the need for mutual assistance, for mutual protection against harm and injury – will tend to regulate an individual's actions without the need for any altruistic 'beneficence' in the individual's motives (Smith 1759: 188–9). Social utility can be assessed through the hypothetical calculation of a 'cool, and impartial spectator' as a kind of objective and disinterested gauge of what is morally permissible (Smith 1759: 79).

For Bentham, a better moral mechanism was the Utilitarian principle of testing a course of action by the 'greatest happiness of the whole community' that would derive from it (Bentham 1952: 91). Without resorting to the facility of a moral imagination, Bentham tried to make moral judgement a straightforward calculus of maximizing the benefit of an action for the largest group of people – or, to put it another way, minimizing the pain for the smallest group: 'Rule: In case of collision and contest, happiness of each party being equal, prefer the happiness of the greater to that of the lesser number' (Bentham 1952: 91–2). J. S. Mill offered a refinement of this Utilitarian moral calculus: refuting human selfishness which is responsible for 'most of the great positive evils of the world', Mill affirms instead that 'the happiness which forms the utilitarian standard of what is right in conduct, is not the agent's own happiness, but that of all concerned' (Mill 1910: 13–6). In this sense, Utilitarian morality refuted the need for any transcendent or nobler moral impulse in man (such as might come from religious edict or a higher moral standard possessed by some), arguing that social interactions and processes would inherently tend to moral ends just from the cooperative and interactive nature of human society.

The moral theories of Smith, Mill and others were developed in the context of (and parallel with) the development of modern capitalist society, their moral reasoning and calculus predicated on a world in which collective moral codes (principally the authority of the Church in the Western world) had become increasingly replaced by individual choices within the mechanisms of the market. The scenario laid out in *Interstellar* is an exaggerated version of the modern economic premise of limited resources and unlimited wants. Klotz (2019: 285) goes so far as to say that time travel in this film resembles derivatives and futures trading, and Professor Brand's juggling of Plans A and B is 'based on a hedging strategy'. Space travel – whether to find a new inhabitable planet or to establish space stations – could represent late capitalism's 'tendency toward globalization' as it abandons 'saturated' and 'exhausted' markets for new ones (Klotz 2019: 284). If the Professor and Mann in this scenario represent economic elites who base their actions on privileged (but ultimately still imperfect) knowledge, then Cooper and the crew of the Endurance represent the common man in the neoliberal social order who has to make individual decisions based on limited knowledge, but whose actions nevertheless have broader (and often unanticipated) social consequences. As in *Inception*, the ideology of the market influences everyone, whether or not they are aware of it.

In the Nolan films of this era like the Batman trilogy and *Interstellar*, we see a greater focus on the morality of individual actions vis-à-vis the public good. In so doing, Nolan interrogates the assumption that Utilitarian morality is immanent, auto-regulatory or easy. The moral dilemma in Nolan's films takes on a Malthusian, zero-sum severity – there seems to be no solution that does not involve a painful sacrifice of some individual or groups of individuals – but also a Utilitarian reasoning, the weighing of relative benefits. Protagonists are often placed in a moral dilemma where their interests – not just their individual survival, but the good of their own loved ones – are placed in zero-sum conflict with that of others further removed, such as colleagues or strangers. In addition, Nolan's postmodernist sensibility continues to see knowledge and interpretation as problematic, thus exacerbating the moral calculus and decision.

In *Interstellar*, this moral dilemma confronts several characters. Professor Brand, convinced he cannot solve the payload equation, has to make the choice to save the 5,000 human embryos while sacrificing all of humanity. Dr Mann and his fellow explorers effectively have to hazard their lives in order to find a habitable planet that will save humanity – all die in the course of their missions, and Mann is only able to (temporarily) escape his planet by faking the data in order to get the Endurance to come to his planet.

Cooper has to sacrifice being with his daughter to go on a mission which (he is convinced) will ultimately save her and the whole human race. Later, after Mann's treachery means that their fuel and bioresources have been compromised, Cooper has to sacrifice himself by leaving the Endurance in the Ranger module, to face likely death in the wormhole, in order for Brand to be able to fly herself and the embryos to Edmund's planet. Brand for her part faces the earlier dilemma of choosing to prioritize either Mann's or Edmund's planets, with the former choice (enforced by Cooper) meaning that she would have to forego a possible reunion with her love interest Edmunds. Nolan is careful to set up these moral struggles by establishing a zero-sum world, where constrained resources mean either-or choices rather than both-and, or even partial compromises: it is worth noting that at the end of the film, after humanity is rescued and huge technological advances come from the data that Cooper is able to send to Murphy, such constraints are no longer part of the film's premise. Cooper is able to commandeer a ship to go and look for Brand (stranded with the embryos on Edmund's planet), with the suggestion that rescue and return to the orbital world would be possible.

Interstellar and indeterminacy: The wormhole of epistemology

A further complication to the moral dilemmas Nolan sets up comes from the familiar theme of unknowability and uncertainty, here given a science fiction twist. Professor Brand is compelled to choose Plan B because he does not have the data on the wormhole that would allow him to solve the payload equation to transport and save all of humanity. This in turn causes him to lie to Cooper and all the others involved in NASA's rescue efforts, so that Cooper makes his choice to leave Murphy and his family based on wrong information – on the premise that Plan A would be possible if a habitable planet could be found. The Endurance team chooses to go down to Miller's planet because of wrong data that suggests that Miller is still alive (when in fact her module had already been destroyed by a giant wave) – data that is correct in the wormhole-affected time frame of Miller's planet but is already false in the time frame of the Endurance's crew. Later the crew decide to go next to Mann's planet based on the positive data he has been sending, only to find after they land that Mann has falsified data in the hope of getting rescued.

The wormhole is the film's McGuffin to bring together Nolan's theme of uncertain and unreliable information. The gravitational black hole of the wormhole distorts time for different parties in different points relative to it, thus negating the truthfulness (or at least the reliability) of data that Miller's probe sends. Once on the other side of the wormhole, the Endurance is unable to send data back to earth, thus preventing Professor Brand from completing his equation and thus also prompting his big lie about the possibility of a Plan A. In one of his recorded messages that reaches the Endurance belatedly, Tom muses on 'all these messages just drifting out there' – a figure for the 'purloined' communications that is a consistent theme in Nolan's films. This epistemic uncertainty created by the wormhole thus enforces the zero-sum scenario in the film, since it compels individuals to make (uncertain) choices that consume precious resources like time and fuel and ensures that each course of action (chosen by or to benefit one party) must necessarily come at the cost of the desires or interests of another.

In this moral laboratory created by the wormhole's influence, human nature – as typically in Nolan's films – proves to be unknowable, not only to others, but even to the self. Professor Brand is perhaps the most obvious example of this, and in summing up the Professor's lie, Mann couches it in Utilitarian terms, as a 'sacrifice' of his own morality and humanity to 'save the species'. The Professor is thus another of Nolan's protagonists – like Dormer in *Insomnia*, like Cobb in *Inception* – whose intended ends appear to justify immoral means. Yet it is by no means clear that Professor Brand's lie was justified: his own deathbed anguish when he confesses to the lie suggests that the moral conflict was not resolved even after his plan (in sending out the team with the 5,000 embryos) was accomplished.

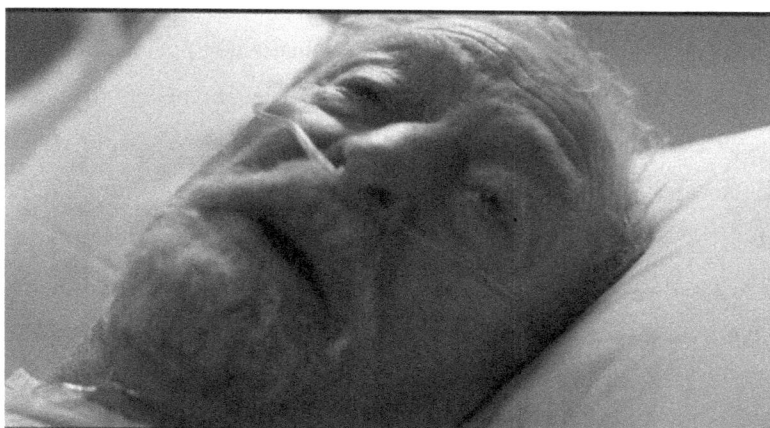

FIGURE 7 *Professor Brand's anguished confession of his lie on his deathbed. Interstellar (2014), directed and written by Christopher Nolan. USA: Paramount Pictures, Warner Brothers, Legendary Entertainment, Syncopy, Lynda Obst Productions.*

He dies quoting a phrase ('do not go gentle') from his favourite lines from Dylan Thomas' poem, which could be interpreted as a regret at his 'gently' accepting the destruction of the earth-bound human race rather than fighting for its survival (as Murphy and Cooper do). Professor Brand's actions reveal some of the problems of the ends-justification morality: firstly, ends-analysis depends on one's available data, and the interpretation of that data. Since the Professor's data is flawed (by the lack of data on the wormhole), so too is his analysis that there is no way to solve the payload equation and save the earthbound human race. The film makes this clear, by showing the happy consequences of a successful plan A after the Professor's death.

Secondly, ends-justification does not justify any means whatsoever to that end; it merely rationalizes the end as an important part of the moral calculus – but the means still have to be included in that moral reasoning. The pioneers of Utilitarian morality vehemently reject the idea that immoral means could serve moral ends. Smith's *Theory of Moral Sentiments* maintained that, while positive affection and altruism were not necessary for social order and benefit to obtain, what was required was a sense of 'justice', that one's behaviour would be acceptable to the hypothetical 'impartial spectator' (Smith 1759: 182, 189). Professor Brand's actions of lying to Coop and everyone else would not pass Smith's test of the individual being able to 'look mankind in the face' after pursuing a particular course of action (Smith 1759: 182), as the Professor's own evident shame at his deathbed confession suggests. J. S. Mill likewise distinguishes Utilitarian morality from cynical 'expediency' and insists that Utilitarianism has 'all the sanctions which belong to any other system of morals' (Mill 1910: 25). Like Smith, Mill believes that social ties and processes – 'the social feelings of mankind; the desire to be in unity with our fellow creatures' (Mill 1910: 29) – not only ensure the most beneficial ends, but also that the means to those ends are consistent with harmonious social relations. Both Smith and Mill would have found abhorrent Professor Brand's actions which alienated his fellow man – the NASA researchers he occupies on a false project, the Endurance crew that he sends out on a false premise, the lying he does to even those close to him like his daughter Brand and his surrogate daughter Murphy.

This moral lapse is reinforced by Nolan's familiar technique of doubling. Professor Brand's double is Mann, the only major character who knows that the Professor's Plan A is a lie. Mann is the Professor's vehement moral apologist, arguing that the latter's lie was an 'incredible sacrifice' that was the only way to 'save the species'. In the same way, Mann and the other eleven explorers are also sacrificial figures, knowing that they may well die in the attempt to find a habitable planet to save mankind. Mann, like Professor Brand, is also initially held up as a saviour and moral paradigm: in an echo of how Harvey Dent is described in *The Dark Knight Rises*, Brand refers to Mann as 'the best of us', a 'remarkable' individual who 'inspired the other eleven' solo explorers. As with the Professor, Mann's defining act in the film is a lie: he sends out positive data on his planet so that he will be rescued, even though his planet is uninhabitable. Later, knowing that his lie will be uncovered and that he and the others will effectively be stranded on an uninhabitable planet, he tries to steal the Endurance to prevent Cooper from using it to return to Earth.

Although Mann's cowardice and abandonment of the crew seem a far cry from the Professor's actions, there is enough similarity for us to question the former's moral position as well. Mann begins from an ends-justification position like the Professor's, perpetuating the Plan A lie in order to inspire the others to find a new home for the 5,000 embryos. In so doing, Mann (like the Professor) is effectively abandoning all the rest of humanity stuck on Earth. Mann's later actions merely take these initial means to their logical conclusion: the lie that his planet is habitable seems a continuation of the lie he shares with the Professor, while the abandonment of the crew on his planet echoes the Professor's effective abandonment of the rest of humanity on Earth. Mann can be seen as Professor Brand's logical development, where the ends-justification reasoning could lead him (and others like him) in due course. Reflecting Nolan's constant interest in names, Mann is so named because he is a moral warning for all mankind.

The moral contrast to the Professor and Mann seems to be Cooper, particularly in his relationship with Murphy and with Brand. While both the Professor and Mann are solipsists, making their moral judgements (affecting many others) unilaterally and with clinical detachment, Cooper wants to believe in Plan A because of his social and affective ties to his family and, by extension, to the others on Earth. Cooper's actions are seen to be governed by the 'love' that is one of the major themes of the film. Cooper is able to communicate with Murphy through the wormhole and thus convey the data that allows Murph to save mankind. The key, as Coop explains to TARS, is 'love ... my connection with Murph', manifested in the watch that Coop had given Murphy (into which they code the crucial data) and which she returns to the doomed farmhouse to salvage because of its association with her father. Love is also seen in the film's closing scenes, the aged and dying Murph surrounded by a host of family members, and Cooper commandeering a spacecraft to go rescue

Brand on Edmund's planet. The affections shown by Cooper, Murphy and Brand are entirely consistent with Utilitarian moral philosophy, in that they embody 'the social feelings of mankind; the desire to be in unity with our fellow creatures' (Mill 1910: 29) that for the Utilitarians should guide our moral calculus and will inevitably be aligned with the common good.

Of course, things are never that clear-cut in the worlds of Nolan's films and even this seeming moral polarization is undercut. Information, as always – its uncertainty and unreliability, its susceptibility to differing interpretations – is a major complicating factor. If Professor Brand's lie proves to be the wrong course of action in the final analysis, his decision is understandable under the conditions of information available to him. This is all the more true of Mann, whose early nobility of action is based on a lack of perfect information (about the planet he seeks and about the space-time realities he will come to experience), and whose later treachery is based on his exceptional experiences. As he tells Cooper, 'don't judge me …. You were never tested like I was.' It is in his epistemic limitation that Cooper most resembles both Professor Brand and Mann: he effectively 'abandons' his family and Murphy (as she herself puts it) because of the limited information available to him at the time that he makes the decision to go on the expedition – the lie that he is a part of the Plan A solution to save Murphy and others like her, the unknown distortions of the wormhole that would almost prevent him from returning to Earth in Murphy's lifetime (or ever at all). The epistemic gap is thus also a lack of knowledge of others and of one's self: Cooper's decision to go on the expedition essentially comes about because he decides to 'trust' the Professor. The Professor's own deathbed agonies shows that he is not really prepared to shoulder the moral burden of lying to the whole human race as he thought he was. Mann's turn from hero to treacherous coward likewise shows his lack of knowledge of his own character and what he is (and is not) capable of.

In *Interstellar*, one of Nolan's sly tricks on the audience reinforces this point about flawed knowledge: Professor Brand, fond of quoting lines from Thomas' poem, is heard in a voiceover quoting a long passage of that poem as the crew takes off into space. Those who know the poem will note that the Professor has left out two lines, jumping instead to the well-known 'Rage, rage against the dying of the light'. This elision hints at the various gaps in knowledge – of space, of other people, even of ourselves – that is the fundamental condition of Nolan's universe. Close readers of literature, and of film, will realize that indeterminacy of knowledge, of the self (including self-knowledge), and thus of moral actions, remains a central concern of Nolan's. In such a milieu, conclusive moral judgements on the part of audiences would be as ill-advised as the decisions of characters like Cooper or Professor Brand.

4

On love and one's fellow man: Towards a transcendent morality

From problematic eros to sacrificial love – a progression?

In Nolan's later films, a new theme emerges, one which will play an increasingly important role: the theme of love, not merely the romantic (and often treacherous) attraction between man and woman that is seen in films like *Following* and *Memento*, but a more idealized and devoted love that exhibits constancy and even sacrifice. Glimpses of this can be seen from *The Prestige* onwards. In *The Prestige*, it appears as a minor theme in Borden's love for his daughter Jess, which is all that remains to him after all the other relationships are destroyed. It is also suggested in the relationship between Cutter and Jess, that it is in part Cutter's avuncular interest in Jess's welfare that turns him against Angier and causes him to aid Borden in destroying Angier and getting his daughter back. From *Inception* onwards, the theme of love and its ability to motivate characters' actions comes to play an increasingly significant role.

The appeal of love, for Nolan, seems to be that it stands as a corrective to many of the social evils that are depicted in his films: the ambition and ruthless professional rivalry seen in *The Prestige*, the violent power embodied in corporations in *Inception*, the zero-sum struggle for survival among different groups of people in *Interstellar*, the fallibility of social authority (police, teachers, scientists) in *Insomnia* and *Memento*. To the problems of society, we might add the problems of the self as Nolan sees it: the unknowability of the self (even to the individual himself or herself), the epistemic gaps in information and data, the treachery and deception that individuals practise on each other (and on themselves). Love, as the transcendence of the self, offers an escape from the problems of the self, and of the conflicts of self-interest in society.

This is not to say that Nolan has anything like a rosy and simplistic view of love, or even of human affections in general. Many of his films depict the failure of eros or romantic love. In the *noir* setting of *Following*, the Blonde seduces the Young Man in order to get him to commit the robbery; she does this out of love for Cobb, not knowing that Cobb intends to murder her. *The Prestige* depicts a similar conflation of eros and betrayal, in Angier using his lover Olivia as a spy on Borden, only to have her turn against him for this exploitative act, and fall in love with one of the twins. Nor is marriage an institution that provides a more secure guarantee of faithful affection: in *Memento*, Leonard's wife tests his mental condition, and their marriage, by making him give her an additional insulin injection, hoping that love will triumph over his memory loss. Instead, she dies when Leonard cannot remember giving her the prior injections, and Leonard proceeds to profane her memory (and salvage his own sense of self and purpose) by constructing a false memory in which she dies in the assault and he is her avenger rather than her killer. Borden's marriage to Sarah in *The Prestige* breaks down when she cannot deal with the apparent contradictions in her husband, and commits suicide. In *Inception*, Mal, like Sarah in *The Prestige*, is a woman who cannot cope with the conditions of her marriage – her desire to stay in her limbo version of reality with her husband, and Cobb's inception of the idea that she needs to die in order to wake up – and commits suicide, but not before implicating her husband in her death.

Nolan is well aware of the problems posed by these romantic or erotic relationships. In this he agrees with Bertrand Russell, who observes that the doctrine of 'Romantic love' promulgated by the Romantics in the late eighteenth and early nineteenth century was not only heedless of 'social consequences', but even 'violent and antisocial' (Russell 1945: 681). For Russell, the doctrine of 'passionate love' associated with the Romantics, as a 'solipsistic' emotion that prioritized 'self development' and saw others merely 'as a projection of one's own Self', is ultimately at odds with social affections and social responsibilities (Russell 1945: 681–2). We see this ego-driven and intense emotion in Leonard's use of his wife's memory to drive the vengeance that has become his raison d'être, and in Angier's similar use of his wife's death (and in his use of his supposed lover Olivia to further his competition with Borden). Arguably the same could be said of the Borden twins, who subordinate their relationships with their respective partners to the all-consuming goal of reaching the peak of their profession. For both Nolan and Russell, this egotistical conception of romantic love is of a piece with the rise of neoliberal individualism and self-centred actions in modern society.

If Nolan's views of eros and marriage are quite dismal, his view of general human affections seems little better. Friends, partners and comrades often turn out to be unreliable, deceitful and treacherous. Dormer shoots his partner in *Insomnia*, and is wracked by the thought that he does not know whether or not he intended it. Teddy, the crooked cop in *Memento*, starts out by aiding Leonard – giving him the file on his wife's assault, helping him kill the assailant – but later continually lies to Leonard to feed the latter's desire for revenge and use him for Teddy's own purposes. Mann in *Interstellar*, initially hailed as 'the best' of humanity and a hero, becomes a cowardly traitor who tries to abandon the Endurance crew to save his own life. In *Inception*, where deep feelings are revealed in the unconscious realm of dreams, the team manages to turn Fischer against his friend and advisor Browning, which may reveal Fischer's deep-seated mistrust of Browning in the first place. In addition, the whole dream action in its different levels depicts Cobb's team befriending and seemingly aiding Fischer, but in reality manipulating him to their own ends.

Yet within this litany of betrayals and failed relationships, Nolan's films do contain a seed of affirmation, seen in the enduring faithfulness of certain relationships. The Borden twins in *The Prestige*, however bizarre and unintentionally cruel their romantic entanglements to their respective partners, are steadfastly faithful to each other. The twin who marries Sarah and fathers Jess appears to be genuine in his love for both of them, and remains true in his love even though Sarah cannot understand his (or rather, the twins') apparent vacillations. If Cobb in *Inception* has a highly problematic relationship with his wife, his love for his children is powerful enough to be his driving motivation throughout the film, even if his means to that end are morally dubious. *Interstellar* foregrounds examples of enduring love, firstly in Cooper's love for Murphy that transcends interstellar separation and the relativity of time that sees her ageing and dying before Cooper, and secondly in the love that develops between Cooper and Brand that has the film ending with him flying off to look for her. The film's premise is that it is the love between father and daughter that drives the encounter in Murphy's bedroom which allows Cooper to transmit the crucial data to her. The plot thus reinforces Brand's earlier assertion of the transcendent truth of love: 'some evidence, some artefact of a higher dimension that we can't consciously perceive'.

We can see that there are exceptions to the cynical view of the self and human society that generally appears in Nolan's films. In some situations and across some relationships, Nolan believes that it is possible for individuals to behave better towards others, to escape the selfishness, ignorance, treachery and social exploitation that are the norm in his world view. We have seen that Nolan eschews a crude, ends-justified pseudo-Utilitarian morality – that for Nolan, even the means have to be moral. Does Nolan's theme of love fit into and flesh out this moral system? Is there a pattern in the positive incidents and relationships that amounts to some kind of moral view? What does this say about the relationship of the individual to others – friends, family, society and species? Nolan's later films – the Batman trilogy, *Dunkirk,* and *Tenet* – develop the possibility of a love that provides the basis of moral action.

Crime, corporations and the divided self: The world of the Batman trilogy

The individual's social affections and consequent moral choices come to the fore in the Batman trilogy. Nolan uses the Batman franchise to create a dystopian society, populated by dysfunctional selves, which serves as a moral test for social affections, civic responsibilities, and the (im)possibility of moral choice. Familiar Nolan themes of the vulnerable and unstable self and the epistemic uncertainties in which that self functions, combine with a broader social canvas and more developed social issues than in the early films.

Nolan's epistemic and psychological uncertainty give his Batman a degree of depth and complexity that is not seen in some of the earlier versions, particularly the campy 1995 *Batman Forever* directed by Joel Schumacher (Winstead 2015: 573–5; Schimmelpfennig 2017: 3). Nolan's Batman is part of a later filmic reimagining of superheroes that depicts a 'darker side' of the superhero figure, 'highlighting the humanity and fallibility of these figures and placing their actions under scrutiny' (Johnson 2014: 952). In this sense Nolan's version is closer to the complicated and morally ambiguous Batman of Frank Miller's graphic novel *The Dark Knight Returns*, or to the superheroes in Alan Moore's graphic novel *Watchmen* or Zack Snyder's films *Watchmen* (2009) and Snyder's 2016 *Batman v Superman: Dawn of Justice* (Johnson 2014: 953). Nolan also injects into the Batman trilogy his familiar technique of character doubling that forces audiences to forego simplistic moral distinctions. To this doubling he also adds a technique not really developed in earlier films (which tended to have smaller casts and focused more on the development of a few key characters) but also evident in his later film *Dunkirk*, the use of the public and crowd scenes to convey moral confusion and ambivalence.

The trilogy needs to be viewed as a whole, and tells an entire story arc about Bruce Wayne, from the death of his parents to his assumption of the mantle of Batman to his defeat of the (seeming) final attack from the League of Shadows and finally his retirement. The narrative structure is rather more straightforward than in some of his other films, although there are chronological leaps and flashbacks typical of Nolan's style, as well as the familiar sequences of crosscutting and parallel action. Viewed as a whole arc, the trilogy explores questions of the self in Bruce's development (as he struggles with the loss of his parents and Rachel Dawes, and as he seeks to reconcile the two identities of Wayne heir and masked hero), and also explores moral questions as he struggles with the means to accomplish the goal of ridding Gotham of crime. There are of course audience expectations that derive from this being a blockbuster film about one of the most well-known heroes in the DC Comics universe. Nolan delivers on many of these expectations, including the technological marvels of Batman's devices, fight and chase scenes, and the appearance of known characters like Selina Kyle (Catwoman), Harvey Dent (Two Face) and Commissioner Gordon. Within these blockbuster and superhero expectations, however, Nolan manages to insert the world view and philosophical questions that he depicts in many of his other films.

Society in Nolan's Batman films is a more explicitly dystopian and dysfunctional version of what we see in *Inception*. Gotham city is essentially run by powerful crime bosses who also control the police and politicians. The point is established early in *Batman Begins*, when

Bruce Wayne as a young man attends the court trial of Joe Chill, the mugger who killed his parents. Chill is released from prison on the instruction of the District Attorney's office, which wants him to testify against the crime boss Carmine Falcone. Falcone has Chill killed just outside the courtroom. When Bruce confronts Falcone in a crowded restaurant, Falcone threatens him with a gun and boasts that although a number of high-ranking police and politicians are seated in the restaurant, he would have no hesitation in shooting Bruce in front of all of them. Large corporations are little better, and we see the power of corporate leaders like Daggett in *The Dark Knight Rises*, whose construction companies place the underground bombs that cripple Gotham, and who is able to financially ruin Bruce by hacking into the stock exchange and placing a large number of fake trades in his name.

There is a close link between the corporations and the crime syndicates, with Daggett working with Bane (until the latter kills him), and (in *The Dark Knight*) the duplicity of the Chinese businessman Lau in his negotiations with Wayne Enterprises even as he also works to protect the money of the crime gangs. Schimmelpfennig (2017: 4–5) argues that in Nolan's Batman trilogy, male characters (whether heroic or villainous) are aligned with capitalism through the displayed power of gadgets, 'economic potency', control over others, and of course heterosexual virility. Gotham thrives on capitalism, and there is a very thin moral line between the rich and powerful CEOs and the dominant and successful crime bosses. Even Wayne Enterprises is suspect: on the one hand, Thomas Wayne (in *Batman Begins*) tells the young Bruce about the good works of Wayne Enterprises, including the public transport system it has built. Yet the transport system was constructed with Wayne Tower at its centre, which not only subordinates the public transport system to the interests of Wayne Enterprises, but also symbolically reinforces the dominance of Wayne Enterprises over the public and the city. It is later revealed that the city's water supply is also below Wayne Tower. Ra's al Ghul takes advantage of this design by putting the microwave device on a train to send it crashing into Wayne Tower and exploding the water supply, intending to vaporize Scarecrow's drug to spread it to the population. When Thomas Wayne dies early in the story arc, the power of Wayne Enterprises is easily hijacked for disturbing purposes: in *The Dark Knight*, Bruce uses Wayne Enterprises resources to turn every cell phone in the city into a sonar transmitter and microphone, in order to locate Joker. Even Fox is disturbed by this abuse of power, telling Batman that 'this is wrong', and threatening to resign after helping him this last time. In *The Dark Knight Rises*, once again the dangerous power of Wayne Enterprises is seen in its development of the clean energy device which Miranda Tate (working covertly with Bane) hijacks to turn it into a powerful nuclear device. Just as in *Inception*, in the Batman trilogy corporate power is threatening and dangerous, at best thinly veiled by good intentions.

Another prevalent aspect of society seen in Nolan's films is the failure of authority. This is especially seen in the police, and Nolan's films have several figures – the policeman in *Following*, Dormer in *Insomnia*, Teddy in *Memento* – of policemen whose cynicism, moral weakness or lack of conviction lead to a failure of authority. Nolan develops this theme in the Batman trilogy. Police corruption is seen in figures like Gordon's partner Flass, who openly extorts money from street vendors and moonlights for Falcone, and in the figure of Ramirez in *The Dark Knight*, who is complicit in the kidnapping and death of

Rachel. Where the police are not corrupt they are incompetent or lack conviction, as in the figure of Foley in *The Dark Knight Rises*, a self-serving officer who initially aspires to arrest Batman, and later shirks his duty and hides in his house when Bane threatens Gotham, before finally finding a degree of vindication.

The context of Nolan's version of the Batman story is this demoralized society in which individuals must either cynically accept the status quo and even try to capitalize on it, or else must take action against it at great risk. Those risks include vigilantism and taking the law into their own hands; consequences of action that are unintended or spiral out of control; the sacrifice of one's own well-being and safety, and also that of one's loved ones; and the loss of one's moral compass as actions escape intentions. Some critics indeed have seen Nolan's Batman as an allegory of and even *apologia* for 'counter-terrorism', for 'the use of force in response to global threats in post 9/11 America', and for the 'with us or against us' mentality contained therein (Johnson 2014: 956; Winstead 2015: 581; Russell 2017: 172). Bruce, as Batman, struggles with many of these moral issues over the course of the trilogy. He is not the only one, however, and similar struggles are depicted in other major characters like Jim Gordon, Rachel Dawes, Harvey Dent, Selina Kyle, John Blake and Peter Foley, and even in unnamed characters in crowd scenes. In his Gotham society, Nolan sets up a larger-scale version of the zero-sum moral problem facing Professor Brand and Coop in *Interstellar*.

Bruce becomes Batman because there seems to be no other possibility for justice to be effected in a city like Gotham. The first issue that Nolan's Batman poses is one of free will, and whether it is even Bruce's choice to pursue justice. In all three films, Bruce struggles with the guilt of his parents' death, because his fear of the bat-like acrobats in the opera caused his parents to leave the theatre early and thus get mugged. A further complication is the death of his love Rachel Dawes, whom he fails to save from Joker in *The Dark Knight*. There is clearly an obsessive quality to Bruce's career as Batman, seen in his refusal to listen to the advice of the benevolent father-figure of Alfred. In *The Dark Knight Rises*, Alfred urges a broken-bodied and worn-out Bruce to quit and instead 'find another way' to help Gotham, and threatens to leave Bruce if he persists. Despite his injuries, Alfred's threat, and the loss of Rachel, Bruce confesses that he cannot 'move on'. He continues in his course as Batman, and (later, when he is in the pit prison) is shown to be still haunted by the memories and guilt: about his father, his fear of bats associated with his fall, and the figure of R'as al Ghul. Bruce thus reveals aspects of the obsessive personality seen by other Nolan characters such as Borden and Angier in *The Prestige*, Dormer in *Insomnia* and Shelby in *Memento*.

The trope of falling is significant, and conspicuously depicted in the trilogy. Early in *Batman Begins*, Bruce as a young boy falls into a pit on the grounds of Wayne Manor, is frightened by the bats which will haunt him all his life and is rescued by his father. In *The Dark Knight Rises*, Bruce is consigned by Bane to the pit prison, where he is again haunted by memories of his boyhood fall. Bane, Batman's nemesis in that same film, is associated with the underground world of sewers and tunnels, where he fights and defeats Batman and where he later traps the city's police. As in *Insomnia*, *The Prestige*, *Interstellar* and other films, the descent for Nolan symbolizes the unknown depths of the unconscious self. This is made clear by the frequent chronological jumps at the beginning of *Batman Begins*, with the film moving back and forth between Bruce's childhood (the fall, the death of his parents), Bruce in a Chinese prison, Bruce's encounter with Ducard/R'as, Bruce's training at the mountain retreat of the League of Shadows and Bruce at Joe Chill's court hearing. As R'as tells Bruce, he must 'journey inwards' in order to resolve his guilt and anger. Bruce's journey as Batman over the course of the trilogy is a journey into his past, the motivations for his actions and his emotional and psychological entanglements with others.

Individualism, imitation and influence: Vigilantism and its double

Apart from his confused motives, Batman also raises issues of the morality of means and ends, and of unilateral individual action. Bruce becomes Batman and takes the law into his own hands because he sees that official channels and authority figures fail to do so. However, as the figures of Rachel, Dent, Gordon and others show, the ordinary individual may be prevented from acting morally if society's structures do not permit it. Rachel's struggles against organized crime are ineffectual, and her efforts are arguably even counterproductive. Her attempts at being a lone crusader for justice in *Batman Begins* only succeed in attracting the attention of criminals, and put her in harm's way where on several occasions (at the train station when targeted by Falcone's thugs, at Arkham Asylum when attacked by Scarecrow) she has to be rescued by Batman. Likewise, Dent as the District Attorney and the main official symbol of justice does not succeed in stemming crime, and instead is overcome by tragedy as a result of Joker's attack, and becomes a deranged criminal himself. Gordon is ineffectual as an honest cop in a system full of corrupt policemen, and initially does nothing in the face of his own partner's corruption. While Batman's training and (above all) the technological superiority conferred by Wayne Enterprises' resources make him a more potent force than any of these other would-be figures of justice, this does not answer the question of whether any individual should act unilaterally, without the agreement or endorsement of society.

Nolan calls attention to the moral problems raised by Bruce's vigilantism in several instances. Alfred on several occasions is the voice of reason and common sense, and in *Batman Begins* warns Bruce about 'getting lost' inside the 'monster' of the Batman. Alfred also warns Bruce that acting from personal desires of revenge would only make him a 'vigilante'. In *The Dark Knight Rises*, Alfred tries to dissuade Bruce from continuing his career as the Batman, and suggests that he can still serve Gotham as a public figure: 'the city needs Bruce Wayne, your resources.'

In *The Dark Knight*, we see some of the negative consequences of Bruce's unilateral actions. Among other things, he has spawned a number of copycat Batmen. Bott (2013: 240) argues that 'mimesis … stands at the heart of Bruce Wayne's strategy to inspire good', and indeed not just Bruce, but also Thomas Wayne, Harvey Dent and possibly other characters in the trilogy seek to inspire others to acts of social justice with their actions and example. Yet despite professing an intention to be a 'symbol' and 'example' to others (as he explains to Alfred in *The Dark Knight*), the impact of Bruce's actions on others is unpredictable, and more often than not disappointing even to himself. While on the one hand his example arguably represents a raising of moral consciousness (and courage) among ordinary citizens, on the other hand it is also shown to result in negative consequences. The imitation Batmen are not really effective against the criminals, and in fact get in Batman's way when he arrives to capture Scarecrow. Later in the film, Joker captures a copycat and uses him to stir up public pressure against Batman and to issue an ultimatum that Batman has to 'take off his mask' or ordinary people like the copycat will die. If the copycats are a nuisance and counterproductive, they are a nuisance inspired and legitimated by Batman's own actions: as one copycat asks him at the beginning of *The Dark Knight*, 'what's the difference between you and me?' Apart from the justification of his greater training or resources, Bruce has no more 'right' within civil society to act unilaterally than these copycat Batmen.

Finally, Batman poses the question of whether any means whatsoever can be used to pursue a good end. There are the personal costs of becoming Batman: the sacrifice of his relationship with Rachel (and the strain in his relationships with Alfred and Fox), the deception he has to practise in playing the role of Bruce Wayne the irresponsible playboy and the sacrifice he chooses to make in taking responsibility for Dent's death. We also see the dangerous measures that he takes to fight criminals, and the direct and indirect costs of his actions. In *The Dark Knight*, he comes up with a sonar-microwave device that utilizes and spies on the cell phones of ordinary citizens. Fox is repelled by this 'unethical' and 'dangerous' move, calling it 'too much power for one man', and threatens to resign. At the end of the film Fox destroys the device at Batman's prior arrangement, but this does not change the fact (as Fox recognizes) that Batman has crossed an ethical line in his pursuit of Joker. In fact, Joker actually points out that he and Batman are doubles of each other, saying (in an ironic reference to Cameron Crowe's 1996 film *Jerry Maguire*) 'you complete me.' Joker's argument is that, in allowing ordinary citizens to die in order to protect his identity, and in allowing Dent to publicly lie about being the Batman, Batman is morally no better than Joker, and arguably mirrors the latter's immorality and threat to the public order. There may be some truth in Joker's view, and he and Batman might well be part of a 'real but hostile bromance, a symbiotic relationship … two sides of the same unreal coin' (Dreyer 2009: 81).

Typical of Nolan's technique of doubling, we also see other characters with an affinity to Bruce, and also exploring depths to their selves and confused or mysterious motivations for their actions. Indeed, Batman in many ways is an index of 'the moral complexity of our society' (Johnson 2014: 957). Again, the trope of the descent gives an explicit clue: R'as, Bane and Miranda are all associated with the pit prison to which Bane consigns Bruce in *The Dark Knight Rises*. R'as points to the parallel between him and Bruce when they train together at the beginning of *Batman Begins*: R'as has also experienced loss (of his wife), and has turned to vengeance to give him purpose and a new life. R'as leads the League in his own version of justice, believing that Gotham has become so corrupt that it needs to be destroyed. Likewise, Miranda and Bane share motivations that are a combination of loss and longing (Miranda for her father, and Bane for her), vengeance (for the death of R'as at the hands of Batman) and a desire to impose their version of justice onto Gotham. Alfred's comments on Bane in *The Dark Knight Rises* could easily apply to Bruce as well: on Bane's origins in the pit prison, Alfred says 'sometimes a man rises from the darkness'; and while watching a clip of Bane fighting, Alfred warns that 'I see the power of belief', which parallels Bruce's conviction in becoming Batman to save Gotham. While these characters' goal of destroying Gotham clearly puts them in opposition to Batman, they represent a trajectory of loss and a desire for vengeance leading to an extreme version of justice that arguably mirrors Bruce's own.

Beyond Joker and the characters associated with the League of Shadows, others also double and echo Bruce's trajectory. One of the most significant of these is Harvey Dent as he is depicted in *The Dark Knight*. Harvey is in fact touted as a more legitimate and acceptable crusader for justice than Batman: in a restaurant scene, Bruce and his date Natasha discuss Batman with Harvey and Rachel, and while Dent defends Batman's role as an 'ordinary citizen standing up for what's right', Natasha criticizes Batman's self-appointed vigilantism, and instead speaks up for 'elected officials' like Dent. She playfully asks, 'What if Harvey Dent is the caped crusader?', a comparison which is reinforced later in the film when Harvey confesses to being Batman (in response to Joker's threats) in order to allow the real Batman to continue his work. Both Bruce and Harvey compete for Rachel's affections, which is another link between them, and both are severely affected by her death.

If Harvey is initially held up as a better agent for justice than Batman, a true 'hero' and 'the best' of all the people, his standing deteriorates over the course of *The Dark Knight*. We see a hint of his capacity for violence early in the film when, in a courtroom scene, he disarms and knocks out a witness who threatens Dent with a gun. Later his zeal for justice and campaign against Joker lead him to dubious means, such as when he captures one of Joker's fake policemen (an escaped mental patient recruited by Joker, and wearing the name tag 'Rachel Dawes'), and plays Russian Roulette with him to get him to reveal Joker's whereabouts. His methods alarm even Batman, who stops him by saying that if the public could see Dent at that moment, his good image would be entirely undone. When Rachel dies and Dent is disfigured as a result of Joker's actions, he becomes completely unhinged and goes on a rampage for vengeance, including kidnapping Gordon's family. Yet his transformation into 'Two Face' is really hinted at in his earlier persona, and indeed the nickname (as Gordon explains) comes from Dent's time in Internal Affairs. It is vital to note that as Two Face, his all-means-necessary attempt to get vengeance for Rachel's death and expose the people responsible for it arguably parallels Batman's similarly extralegal methods.

Other characters ostensibly on the side of law and justice also parallel Bruce's descent into obsession and morally dubious means. Jim Gordon is Batman's closest ally on the police force, and as Commissioner of Police should epitomize the legal and official means of checking crime. Gordon initially stands out as one of the few uncorruptible policemen in Gotham, even when his own partner Flass is accepting bribes. Yet in *The Dark Knight* he agrees to maintain the 'lie' of Dent's heroic actions and death, in order to give Gotham the hero he and Batman believe that it needs. This lie allows Gotham to put in place the 'Dent Act' against organized crime, which in *The Dark Knight Rises* has led to the incarceration of most of the city's mob criminals. Gordon's lie is revealed when Bane reads out the former's draft speech (which Gordon had chosen to suppress) denouncing 'Harvey's appalling crime', and releases the prisoners of Blackgate

Prison ostensibly as a means of correcting the procedural injustice of the Dent Act. The idealistic young policeman Blake accuses Gordon of having 'betrayed everything you stood for'. Gordon defends himself by saying that the lie was necessary because official structures had failed and it was only Batman's sacrifice (in taking responsibility for Dent's death) that allowed Gordon to keep his hands clean – a defence that seems to bear some resemblance to Plato's argument that certain 'Noble Lies' are necessary to persuade citizens to make personal sacrifices for the collective good (Wilberding 2012: 130–2). However, Gordon's lie lacks conviction, as shown by the fact that he feels compelled to write (but does not read out) the truth about Dent's actions, and that (when this confession is found and read out by Bane) Gordon's facial expression (like that of Professor Brand's at his deathbed confession) reveals the shame he actually feels at perpetuating this lie. Blake retorts 'Your hands look pretty filthy to me Commissioner', reinforcing that the ends cannot simply justify any means whatsoever, and also that Batman's act of sacrifice does not necessarily exonerate Gordon from the moral burden of being an accomplice to the lie.

At the heart of Nolan's Batman character is the struggle to act rightly in the face of testing, zero-sum circumstances. As Dent says early in *The Dark Knight*, 'you either die a hero, or you live long enough to see yourself become the villain.' It is prophetic of Dent's career, but it could also apply to Batman, who has to take extraordinary actions in the face of the failure of the social system, and in so doing comes close to becoming a 'monster' (in Alfred's terms) or a 'villain' (in Dent's). Nolan's Batman, as well as other characters in the trilogy (and some in his other films as well), illustrates the inherent paradox of the strong individual who struggles with moral action in a free society:

> The narrative of the rebelliously individualistic hero substantiates and corroborates a key sentiment within punishment ideology: the gate keepers of justice are not only allowed but obligated to go outside the bounds of civil conduct in order to protect society.
>
> (Lockhart 2018: 230)

In thus depicting Batman, Nolan could well be raising questions of the proper limits of authority raised by contemporary issues such as the 'Black Lives Matter' movement or the Patriot Act.

Democracy, deceit and epistemic gaps: Public morality in a postmodern world

The Batman trilogy not only raises the spectre of vigilantism and authoritarianism, but also problematizes public morality, the possibility of moral action on the part of the ordinary citizen. One does not need to have superhero resources, or even vigilante aspirations, to be confronted with moral dilemmas in Gotham; in this respect, Gotham society is very much like the postmodern and neoliberal world of the audience. We can thus easily agree with Johnson (2014: 957) that 'Gotham City serves as an ethical testing ground for audience members, too – a site where they can watch the utility of their own morals play out on the screen.'

Nolan is very much concerned with the possibility of moral action in a postmodern neoliberal order, in which protagonists struggle to act meaningfully and morally. The protagonists in the early films function largely as individuals, and social interactions are minimal and usually variations of failed personal (romantic, professional) relationships. In the later films, Nolan applies the moral problems of action in a postmodern world to larger social relationships – what we might call processes of democratic society or the public sphere. Films like the Batman trilogy, *Dunkirk* and *Tenet* depict masses of people, crowded social canvases that were not evident in the early films (and only to a limited extent in films like *Inception* and *Interstellar*). Nolan depicts crowd scenes where the actions of individuals or groups impact the condition of others around them, where the interests of individuals or groups clash in zero-sum scenarios and where freedom and survival for one group can only exist at the expense of another.

A version of the morality of the public good was seen in *Interstellar*, which shows the concrete social implications of the courses of actions advocated by Professor Brand and Mann on the one hand, and Cooper and Murphy on the other. The decision to secretly forego Plan A is manifested in the people's suffering from the worsening ecological disasters that Murphy and Getty witness as they drive to the farm, and the sickness that Tom's family suffers. In contrast, the happy and contented faces of the inhabitants of the space station, and the social solidarity of Murphy's extended family which surrounds her hospital bed, materialize the social consequences of Murph's and Coop's commitment to Plan A.

The Batman trilogy offers more detailed and concrete examples of individual and group action and their social consequences. This is certainly true of Batman, whose actions (above and beyond battling criminals) lead to a complicated network of social consequences, from inspiring imitator vigilantes, to leveraging on corporate wealth to spy on the public's cell phones and create dangerous nuclear devices, to perpetuating the lie about Harvey Dent that strengthens police and judicial powers (but also compromises them with a deceptive foundation). Unlike earlier Nolan films however, the Batman trilogy is concerned about the consequences of the actions of others beyond the main characters, of the ordinary citizens in different positions in society and different social scenarios. This is particularly true in *The Dark Knight*, where Joker functions as a social experimenter who constantly sets up scenarios which pit individuals and groups against each other. Lockhart (2018: 227) calls Joker a 'self-made self', standing apart from the social conditions that shape normal individuals. Joker – almost as an elemental force outside of social conditions – tests those social conditions, seeking to prove his 'counter-democratic' theories of contemporary society (Lockhart 2018: 227). Joker seeks to demonstrate the 'anarchy' and 'chaos' which he believes to be underlying the apparent social order. By this he seems to mean a cynical, Hobbesian view of human nature as entirely individualistic and competitive. The seventeenth-century English political philosopher Thomas Hobbes believed that the natural state of human kind was a 'warre of every man against every man', where consequently 'the life of man' was 'solitary, poore, nasty, brutish and short' (Hobbes 1968: 186). For Hobbes, the only thing that prevented this natural condition from prevailing was the power of the 'Commonwealth' wherein individuals consent to have a sovereign exert authority and control over them, and thus regulate society and the affairs of man (Hobbes 1968: 223). There is something Nietzschean about Hobbes' view of the natural state of man as lacking any inherent or transcendent morality, and dependent entirely on 'Power' to determine that which is honourable or virtuous or worthy (Hobbes 1968: 153–5). Much in the same way, Nietzsche sees social morality as nothing more than a 'herd instinct', and asserts that the 'future of humanity' is dependent on the 'human will', the 'will to power' (Nietzsche 2002: 90–4). Nietzsche would of course disagree with Hobbes on the necessity or desirability of a 'sovereign' power to ameliorate the natural condition of man. However, the Hobbesian and Nietzschean views of human nature share the belief that there is no inherent morality in man nor transcendent moral principle that man should seek out and adhere to.

When Joker tells Batman that under sufficiently dire circumstances, 'these civilized people, they'll eat each other', he is insisting on a Hobbesian view of man in his natural state. Joker puts in play several scenarios to strip away the veneer of civilization to show man in that natural state. He broadcasts a message that every day people will die unless Batman reveals his true identity. This succeeds to a certain extent in turning people against Batman, with even the police shouting out 'No more dead cops' at Harvey's press conference. The situation is only temporarily defused when Harvey steps forward claiming to be Batman. Later Joker broadcasts a message telling the people that unless Reese (the Wayne Corporation employee who threatens to reveal that Bruce is Batman) is killed, Joker will blow up a hospital. This causes several people with loved ones in hospitals (including a policeman, and a bystander outside the TV studio where Reese is escorted out) to try to kill Reese.

Johnson (2014: 959) argues that the citizens of Gotham exhibit a natural and morally defensible principle of prioritizing the interests of those close to them over those more distant in social relations:

> Gotham's citizens act in accordance with the moral philosophy posited by Kwame Anthony Appiah in *Cosmopolitanism*: "Whatever our basic obligations, they must be consistent with our being ... partial to those closest to us: to our families, our friends, our nations ... and, of course, to ourselves" (165). With this claim, Appiah explains that our moral responsibility to strangers does not outweigh our responsibility to those closest to us. While the majority of characters in Nolan's film tend to abide by this basic approach to ethics, the morality of placing the highest value upon personal relationships is complicated by the severity of the consequences, leaving no easy answers for the players in the Joker's games.

Even if it is understandable for the policeman to be more concerned about his wife in the hospital than for the life of the opportunistic blackmailer Reese, to act on this principle causes problems for others in society, particularly under the stress-test conditions set up by Joker. The logical conclusion of this form of narrow tribalism is social chaos, as individuals take the law into their own hands in order to do what they think is right by their loved ones. We see this in Two Face's rampage after the death of Rachel, Miranda's plan to destroy Gotham in revenge for her father, Bane's devotion to Miranda even at the expense of mass murder and so on. It is only Bruce Wayne's intervention (in ramming the police vehicle) that prevents Reese's murder; in saving the life of the man who is blackmailing him, Bruce demonstrates a sense of duty and a vision of society that rises above these narrower interests.

Perhaps the most fiendish of Joker's social experiments, and the one which really calls into question the fissures in our conception of civic duty and public good, is when he plants a bomb on two ferries (one carrying evacuated convicts and guards, the other civilians) and tells the passengers to blow up the other ferry in order to save themselves. As might be expected, there is an angry and vocal clamour by passengers on both ferries to flip the switch that will destroy the other ferry. The civilian ferry takes a vote, which is overwhelmingly in favour of flipping the switch, and the camera focuses on a Black woman who says 'go ahead, do it', while a White businessman-type passenger, saying 'no-one wants to get their hands dirty', takes the detonator and prepares to press the button.

The ferry scene in *The Dark Knight* focalizes Nolan's concern with the collapse of civil society, which is depicted elsewhere in the trilogy.

FIGURE 8 *Scene aboard the civilian ferry, showing Nolan's use of crowd scenes and camera focus on individuals to create fissures in the public sphere. The Dark Knight (2008), directed and screenplay by Christopher Nolan. USA: Warner Brothers, Legendary Entertainment, Syncopy, DC Comics.*

In *Batman Begins*, R'as' master plan to destroy Gotham consists of a drug which brings out people's innate fears and causes them to act violently and madly, and riots ensue when some of it is released in public. In *The Dark Knight Rises*, Bane (in a ploy similar to Joker's ferry experiment) uses the threat that an 'anonymous Gothamite' has the detonator to the nuclear device to prevent people from trying to flee the city. The ploy works so well that the army and police barricade the bridges out of Gotham and prevent people from leaving, effectively putting them in harm's way. When Blake tries to evacuate the boys from the orphanage, the police shoot at him and blow up the bridge. Bane also exposes the lies about Harvey Dent's heroism to strip off the city's veneer of civilization: it is only this 'false idol' that has (through the Dent Act) managed to imprison so many men and stopped people from 'tearing down this corrupt city'. Bane's control of the city, like R'as' drug in *Batman Begins*, results in a chaotic situation where citizens fear each other, the underprivileged riot and turn wealthy citizens out

FIGURE 9 *The mob rising against the rich after the takeover of Gotham by Bane. The Dark Knight Rises (2012), directed and screenplay by Christopher Nolan. USA: Warner Brothers, Legendary Entertainment, DC Entertainment, Syncopy, DC Comics.*

of their homes, convicts (including Scarecrow) run kangaroo courts and sentence policemen, and policemen like Foley are derelict and hide at home.

It is even possible to see in the popular attacks against the wealthy in *The Dark Knight Rises* an echo of the 'Occupy Wall Street' popular protests against economic and corporate elites (Russell 2017: 172).

In keeping with the general superhero conventions of the trilogy, the Hobbesian provocateurs do not entirely win. The businessman on the civilian ferry cannot bring himself to press the switch, and on the convict ferry a menacing-looking tattooed convict takes the detonator from a guard and deliberately throws it overboard. Bane's 'anonymous Gothamite' who holds the detonator and guards fellow Gothamites turns out to be Miranda Tate, who is so intent on revenge for her father that she can hardly be considered an ordinary or common Gothamite. Yet the Hobbesian point is at least partially made: the civilian ferry overwhelmingly votes to blow up the convict one, even if no one wants to actually press the switch, and the convict ferry is agitated enough that control breaks down and the guards cannot effectively function. R'as' drug does show the fear, violence and paranoia in man, and Bane's reign of terror over Gotham likewise shows some of the worse instincts not just in convicts and ordinary citizens, but even in authority figures like the police.

Nolan suggests that such failings in the civil order are not idiosyncratic and dependent on personalities, but are inherent in our social structure. The contrast between the two ferries in *The Dark Knight* is telling: on board the civilian ferry, the decision whether or not to press the trigger that will destroy the other ferry is decided by a popular vote. In contrast, among the convicts, such democratic rights no longer apply, and no vote is taken. The democratic process on the civilian ferry quickly arrives at a solution that is self-preserving, callous of the fate of the other group (especially since, as one passenger says, they are convicts and have 'had their chance' – an argument which ignores, among other things, the lives of the non-convict guards and ferry crew) and overrides the wishes of the civilians who voted against pressing the trigger. The only reason the convict ferry is not destroyed is because the frightened herd instinct on the civilian ferry has a weakness: in a system in which individual voices vote on a collective public good, the execution of that good must still rest in the hands of a strong individual, and no one on the civilian ferry proves strong enough to be the executive power.

Instead of a democracy, the convict ferry depicts something like a sovereign state or dictatorship, where an Alpha convict (depicted as bigger, stronger and more menacing looking than the rest) makes a decision on behalf of all the rest. The sovereign or dictatorial process appears more dangerous than the democratic one – the big convict appears to want to press the trigger – but finally is shown to be the more selflessly humane one, when the convict throws the detonator overboard to prevent temptation. This scene subverts the expected alignment of humanity, civility and morality with the democratic process carried out by the civilian group. Not incidentally, it also inverts racial and social stereotypes, where the humane action is conducted by the large Black convict, and the selfish and destructive action is proposed (although not finally executed) by the White businessman type. Underneath the frenetic cross-cutting action and suspense of the ferry scene, Nolan plants a view of democracy and individual rights that is highly disturbing.

Of course, the positive outcome of the ferry experiment is highly contingent: the Black convict turns out to be self-sacrificial and benevolent (when he could have seized the detonator and activated it), and on the civilian ferry the unwillingness of any individual to step forward and take the heavy responsibility for carrying out the unpleasant will of the majority leads to another positive outcome. However, Nolan's inversion of audience expectations is nevertheless unsettling, the more so because it is reinforced by other suggestions of the limitations of civil society elsewhere. It is significant that many of the villains are adept at the use of media and the manipulation of the masses. In *Batman Begins*, Scarecrow's mass hallucenogenic drug allows R'as to manipulate the people and cause widespread panic and riots. Joker is a master of media, and repeatedly uses it to reach out to the masses and appeal to their fears and tribal interests. We see this when he uses a TV broadcast to mobilize the crowd to pressure Batman to reveal his identity (with the threat of ordinary people dying until this happens), or when he calls for the public to seek out and kill Reese (threatening to blow up a hospital otherwise). In both cases he is highly effective at stirring up the mob and firing up sectarian interests. In *The Dark Knight Rises*, Bane announces his 'liberation' of Gotham at a football stadium after interrupting a game. Later he makes what looks like a rally speech in front of Blackgate prison, revealing the lie behind the Dent Act, and stirring up not just the convicts but also the public to anger at 'the powerful'. Nolan's villains exhibit strong demagogic abilities, while the masses show their susceptibility to these measures to create sectarian clashes and revolts against authority. In this manner the Batman trilogy presents 'a view of noir America within the neoliberal world order' (Russell 2017: 173). It is a view which invites questions about individual freedom (and its limits) in a democratic society, about our actions and choices and their social costs, about the allure but also the costs of authoritarianism, and about the thin line between social 'good' and 'evil' – questions for which the films offer no easy answers.

Moral mitigation: The possibility of transcendence

Where the Batman trilogy marks a different vision of the self and society from earlier Nolan films is in its vision of the possibility of moral mitigation. This is perhaps to be expected in a blockbuster superhero film, where audiences expect a final uplifting triumph of good over evil. Moral mitigation is also found in the non-superhero films *Interstellar*, in the 2017 *Dunkirk* and the 2020 *Tenet* (all of which appeared after the Batman trilogy), but not in the earlier Nolan films, which suggests that it was a perspective that evolved later in Nolan's career as a filmmaker.

Moral mitigation takes the form of the individual, faced with a zero-sum decision and with little means to effect a positive outcome, mitigating the moral and effective cost by sacrificing one's own interests for the greater good. It clearly does not apply to Nolan's earlier films, with their patently self-interested characters. Leonard in *Memento* and Dormer in *Insomnia* may offer moral justifications for their actions (respectively to find his wife's killer, and to prevent the release of convicted killers), but these justifications are flawed not only because of the immoral actions involved, but also because their moral justifications depend on self-deception and a lack of self-knowledge which render those justifications unreliable. The main characters in *The Prestige* and *Inception* are all morally suspect, driven by professional ambition to take whatever means are necessary to complete their missions and fulfil their ambitions.

It is only with *Interstellar* that we begin to see the theme of moral mitigation emerge in Nolan's work. Although all the characters in this film are confronted with the same constraints and limitations, the same zero-sum choices, it is still possible to identify Cooper (and to a certain extent Murphy and Brand) as the moral centres of the film. Cooper's initial decision to join the expedition may be clouded in part by his personal desire to become an astronaut (and of course by Professor Brand's lie), but he does not act immorally to accomplish this, and in fact sacrifices himself by jettisoning himself in the Ranger so that Brand and the Endurance have enough fuel and life support to reach Edmund's planet. Professor Brand and Mann die alone (emotionally and physically, respectively), symbolizing their alienating actions, whereas Cooper and Murphy – he in his connecting love for Murphy and for Brand, she on her deathbed surrounded by loved ones in stark contrast to Professor Brand – symbolize 'the social feelings of mankind; the desire to be in unity with our fellow creatures' that John Stuart Mill (1910: 29) saw as a key criterion of Utilitarian moral philosophy.

Taking further this distinction between Professor Brand and Mann on the one hand, and Murphy and Cooper on the other, we might say that the former show the dangers not only of any-means-necessary moral reasoning, but also of selfishness – that bugbear of Utilitarian theories of social good. Mill criticizes the condition of 'caring for nobody but [oneself]', and goes on to say:

> To those who have neither public nor private affections, the excitements of life are much curtailed, and in any case dwindle in value as the time approaches when all selfish interests must be terminated by death.

(Mill 1910: 13)

While Mann's selfishness is obvious, it could be argued that Professor Brand also exhibits a more subtle form of selfishness, in bending others to his will and making a colossal decision that will affect all of mankind. In telling Cooper 'I'm asking you to trust me', the Professor places his person and authority solely at the centre of the future of the human race – a future represented in his mind, not by the 'social feelings' of 'fellow creatures' emphasized by Mill, but the abstract potential of 5000 human embryos.

This reading of morality in *Interstellar* provides a basis for a similar reading of the Batman trilogy as well, and allows us to read the film's moral differentiation between the trilogy's many doubled characters. Nolan's 'dark' depiction of Batman (in contradistinction to some earlier versions, especially Schumacher's), his evocation of moral complexities through doubling and other features, actually makes it difficult for audiences to align themselves morally with Batman. Certainly Nolan's Batman crosses a number of moral lines, and the trilogy is as much about causing audiences to acknowledge and think about Batman's moral lapses (and the problems of public morality) as it is about offering a final justification for Batman. In the final analysis, if there is any moral redemption in Batman, it consists not in his purity of motives, nor in his methods, nor in any clear opposition to the villains. Rather, it lies chiefly in the virtue of selflessness. In this we have to disagree with Johnson (2014: 964), who sees Batman's only guiding moral principle as his antithesis to the extremism and desires of the villains he combats: 'Consistently rejecting values without replacing them, Batman becomes a type of moral vacuum or void.' We also have to disagree with Bott (2013: 245), who (based primarily on *The Dark Knight* rather than the trilogy as a whole) sees Batman as 'an anti-Christ figure' because of his creation of the lie concerning Dent, and his perpetuation of the cycle of violence in which he is locked with Joker and other villains.

What finally distinguishes Batman from both the villains and other would-be heroes is his ability to surrender his obsessions, envisioning a social order in which he is not central or perhaps even necessary. His service to Gotham, by the time of *The Dark Knight*, is disinterested and unself-motivated, which he proves by his championing of Harvey Dent as a symbol and agent of justice to replace himself. Batman's willingness to become the scapegoat for Two Face's crimes, in order to preserve the myth of Harvey Dent, is no doubt compromised in its means, but does show Batman's willingness to sacrifice his own standing for what he (mistakenly) believes to be the public good.

Nolan's Batman over the course of the trilogy is depicted as a figure who moves from brokenness and a desire for vengeance, to finally being a figure of selflessness and sacrifice. A mark of that sacrifice is his willingness to become different things – hero, vigilante, billionaire playboy, recluse, villain, martyr – as dictated by the needs of his society. At the beginning of *The Dark Knight Rises*, Bruce seems to have retired from the role of Batman, until he is convinced (in agreement with the views of others like Gordon and Blake) that Gotham needs him. The audience sees Bruce's broken body which he painfully rehabilitates (with the help of enhancements courtesy of Wayne Corporation) in order to return to the role. When Catwoman pleads with him to leave Gotham together with her before the climactic battle in *The Dark Knight Rises*, telling him that he has already 'given … everything' to the people of Gotham, Batman's reply is 'Not everything. Not yet.' Batman almost fulfils this suggestion of dying for the people of Gotham, when he flies off with the nuclear device and is believed to have died in the explosion. Symbolically he has died, a funeral is conducted for Bruce Wayne, and the scene with Bruce, Selina and (at a separate table) Alfred at the café in Florence signals the end of not just Batman, but also of Bruce Wayne's identity and his life in Gotham city. In the final glimpse of Bruce's life with Selina at the end of *The Dark Knight Rises*, Nolan offers us a hint of what had been sacrificed or held in abeyance until his duty to society had been fulfilled.

In this sense Batman is a contrast to individuals like R'as, Joker, Bane and Miranda, all of whom are so closely invested in their projects of justice-by-destruction that they are incapable of being objective and letting go. While they all show no fear of dying in the course of fulfilling their plans, this is distinct from selflessness and sacrifice. Their single-minded pursuit of their goal means that the fulfilment of that goal and the gratification of the self are identical. Their judgements on the moral failures of society are incidental to the fulfilment of their personal desire, which is to impose their own particular visions of chaos on Gotham. Their actions are immoral not just because they cause death and destruction. Nor are their actions validated because they also happen to kill and thwart the careers of evildoers (Joker kills Gambol and burns the money of the crime lords, while Bane kills the criminal financier Daggett). For Nolan, the ultimate moral distinction between Batman and his antagonists (despite the other factors that muddle the differences) is Batman's willingness to sacrifice personal desires in order to give society what it requires.

If selflessness is a moral test, it is one that Gotham's 'hero' Harvey Dent ultimately fails. While he is initially depicted as a heroic public servant, and even a worthy replacement for Batman, when he actually realizes the costs of personal sacrifice – the death of Rachel and the end of his hopes for a life with her – Dent becomes consumed by the selfish desire for vengeance. In contrast, other characters arguably pass this moral test, although perhaps not to the extent that Batman does: Gordon persists in fighting crime although we are told in *The Dark Knight Rises* that his wife has taken the children and left him after the traumatic events of *The Dark Knight*. Foley overcomes his initial cowardice and selfishness to fight alongside his men, and gives up his life in the process. Selina Kyle, despite initially intending to take the 'clean slate' software and escape after clearing the midtown tunnel, unexpectedly returns to fight alongside Batman, although this is complicated by her growing romantic feelings for him, and remorse at her earlier betrayal of him. There are also glimpses of moral victory in other characters, for example the Alpha convict who throws away the detonator on the ferry in *The Dark Knight* even though he believes this will mean his death; or the policemen and special forces soldiers who risk their lives (and in many cases die) to fight Bane in *The Dark Knight Rises*.

Dunkirk: Courage and moral choices in a historical crisis

Bott (2013: 246–7) observes that the audience reception to *The Dark Knight* was largely to see Batman as a 'Christ figure' who embodies 'the enduring power of the sacrificial impulse' – a reading that Bott himself disagrees with. We can compare George Faithful's reading (2014: 412–15) which, while accepting 'Batman's role as a Christ figure' in (almost) giving up his life to save Gotham, sees this as part of Nolan's 'pseudo-Gnosticism' which conceals the deeper truth (that Gotham society may not really be worth saving) by presenting saving illusions in its stead. Both these readings weigh Batman's sacrifice against the deceit he practises on society (a society which is itself rife with deceit and corruption), and come down on the cynical side by reading Nolan's Batman as primarily an illusory symbolism, a sop offered to shore up society's fragile and inherently fractured structure.

Yet when viewed within Nolan's body of work as a whole, and in terms of thematic progression, Batman does seem to point to a redemptive vision which may be hard-won and scarce, but which can still be found in the society that is depicted. *The Dark Knight Rises* equally supports the alternative reading, that Bruce fakes Batman's death not to perpetuate the heroic lie of the heroic Batman alongside that of Harvey Dent, but because his personal example has in fact been effectively sown and taken root. The corrupt police force we see in *Batman Begins* by the end of the trilogy has been tested in the crucible by rising up to fight Bane's forces. The lie about Harvey Dent has been exposed by Bane, and Gordon – purged of any further complicity in it, although not exonerated for his past actions – is now a humbled and more experienced person ready to assume the leadership of the police. Blake is poised to take up Batman's mantle as the superhero Robin. Even other characters like the passengers on the ferry in *The Dark Knight*, and Selina Kyle at the end of *The Dark Knight Rises*, have played their role in overcoming self-interests in order to serve their fellow man. This reading of the moral redemption in the Batman trilogy is corroborated by similar themes in the later films *Interstellar*, *Dunkirk* and *Tenet*. Nolan is not denying the fraught and contingent nature of moral action, and the pervasiveness of the social conditions of doubt and deception, self-interestedness and factionalism. Despite these pervasive conditions, his later films depict glimpses of sacrifice and atonement that are arguably a qualified postmodern version of heroism.

Dunkirk (2017) is unique in Nolan's oeuvre in being based on an historical event, and in being a war film. The large social canvas and epic scale of the action is entirely different from the close focus on the psychology of a few characters that we see in the early Nolan films, but later films like *Inception*, the Batman trilogy and *Interstellar* prepare audiences for some of the blockbuster elements of *Dunkirk*. As for the historical war film element, Nolan seems to find in the story of the British evacuation at Dunkirk a suitable event to express his familiar themes of misinformation, social conflicts and zero-sum scenarios, and the possibility of moral action arising out of this.

Nolan in commenting on *Dunkirk* makes it clear that he is concerned with 'suspense' and 'survival', and not the kind of cinematic action and carnage of Spielberg's 1998 film *Saving Private Ryan* (Lang 2017). Nolan also avoids invoking the towering figure of Winston Churchill so as not to get 'bogged down' in politics (Furness 2017), thus starkly differentiating his film from political dramas such as the 2002 *The Gathering Storm* directed by Richard Loncraine, or the 2017 *Darkest Hour* directed by Joe Wright. Instead, what Nolan wanted to show was 'the courage of ordinary citizens who got in these small boats to rescue people' (Lang 2017). Nolan also explains what attracted him in the historical event of Dunkirk:

> Dunkirk is a story that British people were raised on – it's in our bones. It's a defeat... and yet a defeat in which something marvelous happens. It has an almost biblical, primal sequence to it. Needing a miraculous rescue, and getting it. It's a fascinating tale not of individual heroics but communal heroism. The distinguishing feature of Dunkirk is the coming together of a community.
>
> (Grant 2017)

In such comments we can see the relevance of Nolan's version of the Dunkirk story to the vision of moral courage and the possibility of a cohesive civil society that emerges in his later films.

This is not to say that *Dunkirk* omits the dark picture of the self and the cynical vision of society that are so prominent in Nolan's films as a whole. The historical crisis of Dunkirk allowed Nolan to show man at his most frightened, selfish and internally riven, and society at its most fragile and fragmented. Selfishness is rife as the soldiers assembled on the beach all try to ensure their survival. Long lines of soldiers awaiting evacuation, the lack of sufficient navy ships to take them all, and German fighter planes and the threat of the encroaching German army, create several zero-sum scenarios familiar from Nolan's other films.

Scenes of self-interestedness abound, as when Tommy and Gibson opportunistically snatch up a stretcher with a wounded soldier in order to try to get a place on the hospital ship. On the way to Dunkirk, civilian sailor Mr Dawson rescues a Shivering Soldier, who insists that they go back to England, and turns violent when Mr Dawson insists that they are going on to Dunkirk. He knocks down the teenage crew member George, who suffers a head injury and goes blind, and later dies of his injury. When Tommy, Gibson and Alex join a group of soldiers (the Highlanders) on a beached Dutch boat, German soldiers shoot holes in the boat so that it threatens to sink under its load in the rising tide. Alex and the Highlanders discover that Gibson is really a French soldier who had stolen his uniform and dog tags from a dead British soldier, and they try to force him out of the boat in order to lighten the load – this despite the fact that Gibson has helped save the lives of both Tommy and Alex earlier.

There are also signs of tribal loyalties as the soldiers band together according to nationality and army unit in an attempt to strengthen their positions vis-à-vis others. At the beginning of the film, when Tommy retreats past a French fortified position, the French soldiers contemptuously push him on his way and away from them. Later on the Mole, the British Warrant Officer responds in kind when he repeatedly tells the French soldiers that places on the evacuating navy ships are only for English soldiers. When Tommy tries to join a queue of soldiers awaiting evacuation on the beach, the soldier ahead of him points to his Grenadiers regimental badge as a signal to Tommy that he does not belong there. On board the riddled Dutch boat, Alex closes ranks with his Highlanders and singles out the French soldier Gibson as the first to be sacrificed in order to lighten the load (even though Tommy points out that the French are allies). Alex also tells Tommy (who is English but does not belong to the Highlanders) that he is next in line in case they need to jettison more weight.

Nolan also finds a way to express his theme of epistemic uncertainty clouding the individual's decisions, in the chaos and confusion of war, and the lack of knowledge of what lies ahead of and around one. The German army is always reported to be approaching, but it is never known how close they actually are, and thus how much time the retreating British actually have. Individuals thus act on the worst-case assumption that the Germans are coming down on them at any minute, and this exacerbates the selfishness and desperation of individual actions. Epistemic uncertainty is symbolized in the faulty fuel gauge of the pilot, Farrier, who thus has to make a difficult decision (whether to stay and protect the troops, or to head back to England before he runs out of fuel) based on imperfect knowledge. Farrier is not even certain at that point that it is the fuel gauge, and not something more dire like a leaking fuel tank or burst fuel line. Nolan also finds a way to work in some of the non-sequential storytelling techniques more evident in some of the other films: events occur as they are seen by different characters, not always in the sequence in which they occur. From the air, Farrier sees the Dutch boat sinking before the audience (later) sees how Alex, Tommy, Gibson and the Highlanders get on the boat, and the various misadventures and confrontations leading to the boat sinking and Gibson drowning. Likewise, the audience from the perspective of the fighter pilots see Fortis Leader and Collins both shot down, leaving Farrier as the lone pilot, before later seeing (from the perspective of Mr Dawson on his boat) two Spitfires (meaning that this depicts a time before Collins is downed). The characteristic Nolan technique of non-sequential storytelling, in this film, reinforces the confusion of wartime conditions and the unreliability of information and sightings.

Near the end of the film, several poignant episodes further reinforce the confusion and misinformation governing the soldiers' actions. When the rescued spitfire pilot Collins gets off Mr Dawson's boat at Weymouth, another evacuated soldier spots his RAF uniform and shouts angrily at him, 'Where the hell were you?', unaware that Collins had been shot down defending the troops from German fighters. As Alex and Tommy prepare to take the troop train out of Weymouth, Alex is overcome by shame at the British army's retreat, and perhaps also guilt at his earlier desperate hostility to Gibson and Tommy. He believes that the man handing out blankets to the soldiers refused to look him in the eye, not realizing that the man is actually blind. Later as the train pulls into a station Alex is ashamed to look at the civilian crowds gathered there, assuming that they will despise the soldiers for cowardice, and is pleasantly surprised when they instead cheer the troops. When the Shivering Soldier at one point guiltily asks after the condition of 'the boy' George, Peter offers him the saving lie that George is okay when he is in fact dead. Perhaps the most poignant example is when Peter gets the local newspaper to print a story that George had died as a 'hero at Dunkirk', instead of the ignominious truth that he died from a fall when the Shivering Soldier panicked and struck out wildly. This episode is a variation on the saving lie of Harvey Dent's heroism, although in the lie about George's death we do not see the same large-scale negative consequences that we see when the lie about Dent is revealed in *The Dark Knight Rises*. The film closes with Tommy (safely on the train) reading Churchill's parliamentary speech, becoming a voice-over as the camera cuts to the beach and pans over the bodies and military detritus, including a shot of soldiers' helmets that is a visual echo of the masses of Angier's hats created by the indiscriminate copying in *The Prestige*. The audience is torn between the pugnacious determination of Churchill's rhetoric (mediated through Tommy's tentative reading and diffident voice, rather than in the form of Churchill's famous oration in Parliament) on the one hand, and the evidence of the human and strategic costs on the other. Dunkirk as historical event, seen through Nolan's directorial gaze, poses a fundamental question of interpretation, whether it can be seen as a British 'deliverance' and 'victory' or 'military disaster' (in Churchill's terms), or something else altogether.

Nolan is also true to his recurring theme of the unknowable self and the hidden depths which may lie beneath one's actions and ostensible motivations. In this historical war movie, Nolan accomplishes it, not via the psychological depths of *noir* conventions, but rather through the flat psychologies of the characters encountered during this Dunkirk moment. As Nolan's cinematographer Hoyte van Hoytema explains, the film deliberately removes much if not all of the background and psychology of the characters, even the civilian ones: 'We're thrown on the beach with these characters without knowing much about them … Everything comes at you, and it's immediate and visceral. We took away anything personal or sentimental' (cited in Lang 2017). Gibson perhaps best epitomizes this immediacy of action, the subordination of background and personality to the survival imperative: he takes on literally a new nationality and name in an attempt to get off the beach, and the audience knows nothing about his background and the events in his life prior to the time he is introduced onscreen.

When the audience sees Gibson helping others in various ways – using the dodge of the stretcher to almost get himself and Tommy onto the hospital ship, pulling Highlanders out of the water when the ship sinks, stopping to open the door on the sinking destroyer so that Alex, Tommy and others can get out – we cannot be sure how much (within his mixed motives) is due to altruism, and how much a desire to ingratiate himself with the British troops so as to escape detection and be evacuated with them. If it is easy to condemn the cowardly panic of the Shivering Soldier that inadvertently results in George's death, Nolan undercuts this judgement by reminding the audience (via the civilian skipper Mr Dawson) that he is 'shell-shocked' and is 'not himself ... may never be himself again'. When Alex and Tommy, after their series of misadventures, find themselves together on Dawson's boat and then on the train out of Weymouth, they exchange a brief and enigmatic look, which is all that audiences are given to account for their turbulent relationship in which they have both helped each other survive, fought others for a chance to survive, and even faced off against each other.

However, this unknowable nature of the self cuts both ways, and if Nolan deliberately curtails speculation about the motives and background to characters' desperate and ignoble actions, the same is also true of characters' noble and selfless ones. The ultimate mystery that Nolan presents for the audience's contemplation is that of human nobility, selflessness and sacrifice in the midst of fear, misinformation and selfishness. Farrier – his background and character undeveloped, even his features obscured by his flying helmet and goggles (a Nolan allusion to the masked figure of Bane in *The Dark Knight Rises*, also played by Tom Hardy) – is the most prominent example of this. There is clearly an element of selflessness and sacrifice in the depiction of Farrier, and the way in which he continues protecting the soldiers from the air while aware that his fuel is running out and that he will not be able to return to England. After landing, Farrier ignites his spitfire with a flare gun, possibly to prevent its capture by the Germans, although there does not seem to be anything on the emptied plane worth taking. Possibly the act is to evoke the notion of a burnt sacrifice, with Farrier symbolically offering himself up as expiation in exchange for the deliverance of the escaped British soldiers. Tellingly, he makes no attempt to escape, not even to make his way down the beach to where some British soldiers still remain (and were seen cheering his plane as it descended over them).

Although the final scene of Farrier standing before the burning plane as the German soldiers descend on him is the most dramatic

FIGURE 10 *Farrier standing before his burning plane, with symbolic connotations of a burnt offering on a pyre. Dunkirk (2017), directed and written by Christopher Nolan. USA: Syncopy, Warner Brothers, Dombey Street Productions, Kaap Holland Film.*

evocation of the theme of sacrifice, it is far from the only one in the film. There is an element of sacrifice depicted in the figure of Gibson, who although intent on survival, is also seen as the instrument of salvation for others. The fact that Gibson (as disguised Frenchman) is alienated by the British soldiers, almost sacrificed by the Highlanders when the Dutch boat is shot at by the Germans, and finally loses his life when he is the last one left plugging the leaking holes and cannot escape the sinking boat in time, adds to the poignancy of his death. He may not have had the clear intentional selflessness of Farrier, but was instrumental in saving some of the men who later rejected him. Yet another figure is that of George, the idealistic boy who jumps onto Mr Dawson's boat in order to participate in the evacuation of the troops, but who dies ignominiously when he is struck by the panicky Shivering Soldier whom they rescue. The confused, unintended and seemingly meaningless nature of his death only heightens George's tragedy. Peter's saving lie to the local newspaper is a way of trying to make good out of that senseless death; yet perhaps another way in which George's death is meaningful is precisely because of its senselessness, that in his innocence he is an atonement for the diffusive culpability all around him, from the political leaders responsible for the war down to the ordinary soldiers who turn on each other in order to survive.

Nolan in the final analysis is right in saying that *Dunkirk* is a 'fascinating tale not of individual heroics but communal heroism' (quoted in Grant 2017). Nolan neither glorifies war nor tries to redeem the military catastrophe of the historical event. The soldiers' world is one of confusion, the immediacy of fear and the overwhelming imperative to survive, in which there is little prospect of forward planning, much less noble intention. There is indeed something 'miraculous' (in Nolan's terms, quoted in Grant 2017) about the resulting rescue of more than 300,000 British soldiers, given the lack of cohesion, communications and organization evident throughout the film. The 'miraculous' nature of the resulting evacuation, the 'communal heroism' that brings it about, does not rely on each individual acting nobly or heroically – quite the opposite, as the film's individual stories reveal. 'Communal heroism' in this context, for Nolan, seems instead to refer to the way in which the social whole is bigger than the sum of its individual parts, the way in which fear and selfishness in some instances can be evened out and atoned for by sacrifice and selflessness by a few others and in other situations. In de-emphasizing 'individual heroics' (Grant 2017), Nolan insists on Dunkirk as a national event, a victory for the British people as a whole. Within that collective victory, Nolan embeds the abiding mystery of human nature and human society – how the latter can function at the intersection of individual selfishness, tribalism and sectarianism, the failure of interpersonal communication and right information. If *Dunkirk* continues and even enhances the social hopefulness of Nolan's later films like *Interstellar* and the Batman trilogy, it also retains the essential mystery that Nolan sees at the heart of our society.

Tenet: Moral inversions, individual will, and the question of 'faith'

The central premise in *Tenet* is science fiction: temporal inversion and its potential consequences for individuals, society and the whole world. As with the dream state in *Inception* and the quantum possibilities of the wormhole in *Interstellar*, Nolan uses this science fiction premise of time inversion to challenge our fundamental sense of selfhood: what the self knows (about the self and others), the relationship between self and society, and assumptions about causality and morality. Doubling, used in many Nolan films to depict hitherto unknown and unconsidered psychological depths in characters, is literalized in *Tenet* in (among other ways) the form of characters' inverted doubles who chronologically reverse the actions of their originals.

This possibility of reviewing, replaying and influencing one's own actions results in uncertainty and unknowability: thus the Protagonist in Tallinn goes through the turnstile to try to prevent Sator from seizing a piece of the algorithm, only to effectively hand it to him instead. Near the end of the film, the Protagonist still has not figured out that it is in fact he who had recruited Neil (until the latter informs him of this), and that he is in fact effectively the puppet master pulling the strings of various individuals, including Priya. The possibility of chronological inversions not only means that characters in any particular point of time may not fully know themselves (since there is always the possibility that they may in the future go back into the past and affect their courses of action), it also overturns conventional causality, since a future event may not only be the effect of an earlier cause, but it can also be the cause of an inverted intervention that has an effect in the past. In this sense *Tenet* plays out on a global scale a version of Leonard's amnesia in *Memento* (where his polaroids and mnemonics can be both the effect and record of what has happened, as well as the stimulus and cause of what he will do next). There is even a common visual motif between the two films, the image of the bullet's reversed trajectory back into the gun (Newby 2020). If conventional causality is challenged, then so too is conventional morality, which relies on a strict cause-effect relationship where the consequences of one's actions are determinable and must then be considered before executing the action.

In terms of larger structural techniques and devices, *Tenet* draws together many of the features of Nolan's other films. We see the larger social canvas of Nolan's later films, and the ways in which this is used to depict moral concerns of social factionalism and of the individual's relationship to and responsibility for the public good. If *Dunkirk* was a historical film in the sense not just of dealing with an actual historical event, but also in the sense of dealing with the expansive social scale of nations and their destinies, *Tenet* too (notwithstanding its speculative fictional premise) can be called 'historical' in that its moral perspective encompasses nothing less than the whole human race and its standing in space and time. There is even a visual echo of *Dunkirk* in *Tenet*'s Stalsk-12 battle scene, in the lines of 'blue' and 'red' soldiers deploying from and evacuating in their airborne containers, and in the glimpses of soldiers carrying wounded on stretchers. Nolan's narrative disruptions are not as prominent in this film (compared to, say, *Memento* or *The Prestige*), but do make an appearance in the form of the replay of scenes due to time inversion (for example, the Protagonist's fight with a masked man at the Oslo Freeport earlier in the film, which is latter replayed and explained as his fight with his own inverted self; or the repeated scene of Sator's yacht in Vietnam and the interactions between Kat and Sator, which is replayed and explained as Kat's efforts to prevent Sator from killing himself until the algorithm is secured). Nolan's crosscutting technique is very much in evidence, not perhaps to the extent of *Inception* (although both films have exciting corridor fight sequences, Kiang 2020), but evident in the climax of the film in the dual perspective of the blue and red 'temporal pincer movement', crosscut too with Kat's actions on the yacht.

In many ways, and fittingly for Nolan's latest work to date, *Tenet* amplifies the themes and symbols found in earlier films. Threatening and powerful corporations and oligarchs like Cobol and Saito in *Inception* or Daggett and the crime bosses in the Batman trilogy, take on even more frightening form in the arms dealer Priya (who despite her urbane and gracious appearance is a consummate manipulator and ruthless in her desire to kill Kat just to tie up loose ends), and in Sator who has seemingly limitless wealth and resources funded by the future, and who aims at nothing less than the destruction of the present world. Nolan's favourite themes of uncertainty and unknowability are also at work in the depiction of powerful but shadowy agencies and organizations in the film: we never learn anything about the future cartel that is using Sator to try to 'invert the entropy of the world' (as Neil explains). Even the Protagonist's affiliations are murky: at the beginning (in the Kiev siege) he seems to be working for an American organization like the CIA, but his CIA suicide capsule is somehow switched with a sedative, and later Fay tells him that the whole episode was merely 'a test'. By the end of the film the Protagonist declares that Neil and Priya are actually working for him (or rather, for the Protagonist of the future), but the audience knows no more about his affiliation than that of Sator.

One of the consequences of the uncertainty and shadowy power evident in the film is that the line between Protagonist and antagonists blurs. In many ways the Protagonist and Sator are doubles of each other, even while the film's tension and plot depend on the struggle between them. Some of the familiar Nolan devices are at work in this doubling: the McGuffin of time inversion (like the wormhole in *Interstellar* that prevents accurate data from being transmitted) renders present action questionable, simply because there is no way of knowing what future conditions or causes may be effecting or justifying the action in the present. In this sense the struggle between the Protagonist and Sator is ends- and result-blind: for all the audience knows, the Protagonist's cause may eventually lead to greater human suffering and loss of life than Sator's. Certainly both causes appear to be well matched in terms of their methods: both have armies and heavy armaments which they freely use on each other, and both are capable of violence and ruthlessness. The Protagonist and crew (like Batman) even resort to extralegal, extra-judicial measures: they shoot up the Estonian police car, and the Protagonist executes Priya and her henchman to prevent them from executing Kat. Once again, inception – the planting of words or ideas into someone else, with the blurring of causality and the boundaries of the self – seems to be at work. Like the password introduced at the beginning of the film ('We live in a twilight world'), other phrases like 'ignorance is our ammunition' and 'lying is standard operating procedure' pass from character to character, so that it is not clear who originates these sentiments.

In the final analysis, beneath the action-packed struggle and the seeming opposition between the two factions, their moral distinction is a dubious one. The zero-sum proposition – that the saving of the present generation is the dooming of the future one, and vice versa – removes moral absolutes in the struggle between Protagonist and antagonists. If the Protagonist can say to Sator 'each generation looks after its own survival', then this is as much a justification for Sator's future faction as it is for the Protagonist's. Sator's explanation – that the people in the future 'have no choice' for their actions because of the environmental depredations of the present generation – even has the ring of plausibility in the light of real environmental concerns (just as Bane unleashing mob violence against the rich in *The Dark Knight Rises* evokes real concerns about social inequality and the perceived greed of the 'one percent'). The zero-sum condition that is seen in other Nolan films, is no less imperative here, and (especially in the face of epistemic limitations) there are no simple moral decisions.

What *Tenet* shares with Nolan's later films – *Interstellar*, the Batman trilogy, *Dunkirk* – is once again a fragile, almost evanescent notion of heroism based on selflessness and right intentions to one's fellow man. Sator as villain is R'as, Mann, Professor Brand and other threatening visionaries writ large. The selfish arrogance of his actions and motivations is foregrounded in the film: he wants to take the present world with him because he is dying anyway, and (as in his relationship with Kat), 'if he can't have her [both Kat, and the world], no-one can.' Sator arrogates to himself the right to take away the lives of many, just as R'as intends to destroy Gotham because he has decided that it cannot be redeemed, or Professor Brand takes upon himself to lie to everyone and consign humanity to death on a dying planet. The film's depiction of Sator's hubris is hinted at in his name, which is not only the first line of the Sator Square that Nolan evokes in the film's title and elsewhere (including in the art forger's name

Arepo and the name of the corporation Rotas), but also the name of one of the Roman *numina* or gods associated with functions – in this case sowing (Hunt 2019: 147). Sator, in his self-justifying argument over the walky-talky with the Protagonist, actually refers to himself as a 'god' of sorts. This hubris is also ironic, since Sator is more grim reaper than sower, and would even destroy his own seed (his son Max) together with the whole world.

While Sator's hubris causes him to want to destroy the present world with his own death, the Protagonist – no less ruthless in his commitment to his cause – is associated with the preservation of his society and community. The film establishes his selflessness early in the film, when he (in contrast to other captured and tortured agent) refuses to give up his team and organization: as Fay says, 'you chose to die instead of giving up your colleagues.' While Sator is alienated from those around him, including his wife and son, the protagonist forms a camaraderie and community with others like Kat, Neil and Ives. A higher moral imperative also distinguishes this group from the villains: Ives near the end of the film wants to follow orders and kill both Neil and the Protagonist to ensure the algorithm is never recovered, but (unlike Priya) seems to follow a higher moral principle and instead divides the algorithm's components among them and tells them to stay away from him and each other. So too does the element of sacrifice serve as a distinguishing feature: the Protagonist's group, in saving the world without anyone ever knowing it, is arguably 'profound in its selflessness' (Newby 2020). Neil, in the most cryptic but also most poignant part of the film, seems to have resigned himself to a perpetual loop of going back and forward in time at the Stalsk-12 pit, picking the lock and being killed by Volkov and then inverting to open the door for Ives and the Protagonist. His act of very deliberately going back to his fate – 'that's me in there again' – seems even to shock Ives and the Protagonist, with the latter struggling in vain to find an alternative. Neil in this scene has a certain atmospheric similarity with Farrier at the end of *Dunkirk*, who also in very deliberate fashion goes to his fate of capture and possibly death, choosing to do this in order to save more soldiers from aerial attack.

Salvific intentions combine with a hope for a better outcome for humanity – a strand of meaning consistent with the depiction of characters like Coop and Murphy in *Interstellar*, Batman, Gordon and Blake in the trilogy, Farrier and Dawson in *Dunkirk*, and others. This may well deserve the term 'faith', which is used by both Sator and Neil in *Tenet*. This is not to forget the dangers of the 'leap of faith' depicted in *Inception*, that it can also be the justification for reckless and cost-insensitive actions. There is nothing evangelically absolute about Nolan's use of the term – Sator equates the Protagonist's faith with fanaticism, the Protagonist counter-proposes the term 'fate' instead, and even Neil offers 'reality' as a possible substitute. Yet in Nolan's epistemically confused and uncertain worlds, where even the self's own motives and actions are not clear, where betrayal and oppression by others and by powerful social forces are evident, that 'faith'-like element persists, and is the basis of the audience's difficult yet significant alignment with Nolan's heroes and protagonists. 'Faith', in the final analysis, may be something as much for the auteur Nolan to cling to, as for his audiences.

5

Conclusion: Film, philosophy, belief – Nolan's men in the crowd and the 'good will'

British novelist Ian McEwan's novel *Enduring Love* – published in 1997, a year before Nolan's first full-length feature film *Following* – has its protagonist, Joe Rose, express his disappointment when an attempt to reconstruct an event through the accounts of witnesses falls flat: 'We lived in a mist of half-shared, unreliable perception, and our sense data came warped by a prism of desire and belief, which tilted our memories too' (McEwan 2006: 180). Rose's sentiments could easily serve as an apt epigram for Nolan's films, and indeed for postmodern art and meaning-making in general. As we have seen, Nolan's films explore the myriad and subtle ways in which the self functions at the nexus of epistemic gaps, misinformation, mixed and occluded motivations, even wilful self-deception. The self is also the site of external influences, from the mimetic impulse to follow the actions of others, to being swayed by their lies and betrayals, to being controlled by the power and ideology of corporations and consumer culture.

It is worth pointing out, at this juncture, that Nolan's protagonists are almost all male – from the Young Man, to Leonard Shelby, to Dormer, to Bruce Wayne, to Angier and Borden, to Cobb, to Cooper, to Tommy and the other soldiers in the almost exclusively male cast of *Dunkirk*, to the Protagonist in *Tenet*. In the earliest films – Nolan's take on the film noir – female characters play variations on the treacherous femme fatale, and Miranda Tate in *The Dark Knight Rises* as well as Mal in *Inception* seem to be Nolan's return to that type. Later films have significant and more complex female characters, such as Burr in *Insomnia*, Olivia and Sarah in *The Prestige*, Murphy and Brand in *Interstellar*, and Rachel Dawes and Selina Kyle in the Batman trilogy. Yet there seems to be an unmistakable gender differentiation that is worth noting. The characters who exhibit the hollow self that is influenced and shaped by external circumstances, the ones who are tested by (and often fail) moral decisions in postmodern neoliberal society, are generally male. Nolan's female characters by and large escape the moral *agon* experienced by the male characters, and consequently play something of a secondary role to the men. Even the femme fatales operate under some male agency or guidance: the Blonde is a victim of Cobb's schemes, Natalie is placed in her difficult situation (and thus uses Leonard) because of the actions of Jimmy and Leonard, Mal is ultimately the victim of Cobb's inception, Miranda sees herself as the heir of her father's destructive homicidal legacy and Priya essentially operates under the direction of the future Protagonist.

When female characters do undergo a moral test, they have less agency for decision, given the dominant role of the men around them. Murphy in *Interstellar* is the possible exception, as she (like Cooper) is affected by Professor Brand's lie, is tempted by emotional withdrawal from her father, despair, and consequently the abandonment of the Plan A that will save the lives of the Earth community. Murphy has to continue her struggle to solve the Plan A equation, but in this she is dependent on Cooper, who is the more active agent in transmitting the data to her and in eventually returning to her side. A case might also be made for Brand, who is tempted to choose Edmund's planet out of a combination of self-interest and erroneous data, yet she has no real moral test as she is overridden by the other (male) characters. Her voyage to Edmund's planet is also determined by a male character, as Cooper jettisons the shuttle to enable her to complete her voyage; and at the end of the film we see her passively waiting on the planet, with Cooper on the way to rescue her. Selina Kyle over the course of *The Dark Knight Rises* goes from femme fatale who betrays Batman, to sacrificing her interests in order to help him save Gotham. Again it is Batman's persistent forgiveness and faith in her that seems to win her over, rather than a profound moral turn on her part. Thus even when female characters undergo moral testing and struggle with society's postmodern constraints, it is still the men who play the more active role in assisting these female characters towards their course of action.

Nolan displays almost a Victorian gender sensibility, in placing men in the role of the active agent struggling against external forces, either overcoming them to achieve some degree of heroism, or else succumbing to moral corruption. In contrast, women (to varying degrees) play the passive role, their actions (whether for treachery and destruction, or for societal benefit) governed by the men around them. Underlying the apparent agency and power of even the more significant of Nolan's female characters – Murphy, Mal, Selina Kyle – is a gendered sensibility which largely exempts women from the profound moral test that the male protagonists endure, that excuses them from a head-on confrontation of postmodern society's dark aspects. It is a gendered sensibility that is not too far off from the Victorian separation of women for sheltered domestic roles and men for the far more active and influential spheres of government, the military and business (Ittmann 1995: 142–3; Jalland 1996: 98–9).

Since the individual's choices and actions have implications for others, the diminished agency of female characters consequently has a diminished social impact as well. Nolan's films show a recurring concern about the ways in which individual actions impact others in society. This could be at as small a scale as the romantic relationship, the family or the relationship between colleagues; on the other hand, it could be as large a scale as an army, the population of a city, or the whole human race. Nolan's films show a profound mistrust of social processes, given that these are dependent on the choices and actions of flawed and limited individuals. The microcosmic social relationship expands out into macrocosmic ones, and Nolan's films inevitably show a mistrust of neoliberal consumer society, media influence, mob action, corporate power and police and government.

Herein lies the hermeneutic circle of Nolan's vision (a circle aptly visualized in the palindrome 'tenet'): society and the individual are co-causal, and the individual is shaped by social forces, even as his actions impact those in society. If Cobb in *Inception* is ultimately a corporate tool, it is also the inventive ruthlessness of individuals like

Saito, Cobb and his gang which perpetuates that corporate power. Cobb's manipulation of his own wife is of a piece with the team's manipulation of Fischer and his corporation. If the young Bruce Wayne's psyche and subsequent career are shaped by Gotham's crime syndicates and the murder of his parents, Bruce in turn uses Wayne Corporation to obtain his goals, and often in extralegal ways. Bruce's vigilantism may be directed at those who break the law, but there is no denying his resemblance to the extralegal and authoritarian nature of corporate bosses like Earle and Daggett, and villains like R'as al Ghul, Miranda Tate and Bane. Nolan's film techniques, including the use of symbolic and visual doubling, make this resemblance clear.

Nolan's protagonists are ultimately men in the crowd, figures indistinguishable from the masses who live their lives under the influences and within the constraints of an alienating, postmodern and neoliberal society. In this respect he has been consistent throughout his career, and despite his use of quite different film genres. At the close of his first full-length film, *Following*, Nolan offers a visual image that aptly depicts his view of the human condition: Cobb, the manipulator pulling both the Blonde's and the Young Man's strings, is standing on the street facing the camera, with passers-by crossing between him and the camera POV. After a group walks past, Cobb has disappeared – as mysteriously and as unaccountably as he entered the lives of the other characters, with his background and his future actions still unknown both to the audience and to the characters. Although many of Nolan's later characters are more fleshed out and shown with more psychological detail, there remains something of Cobb's flatness and elusiveness about them all – including the Protagonist of Nolan's most recent film, who is not even given a name, and whose affiliations and justifications in the future are never revealed to the audience. One major reason for this is that they are ultimately unknowable to the audience because they are unknowable to themselves. Nolan's films consistently raise questions about the self: its motivations, hidden depths, secrets and self-deceptions. If this self is furthermore the site of external influences – the lies and manipulations of other individuals, the ideologies of consumer culture and neoliberalism – this too is never recognized by the self, and adds to its complicated and unknowable nature. In the final analysis, Nolan's protagonists show more about the condition of living and acting in a postmodern world than they do about any inherent self or true character and motivations.

It may seem that the depiction of men in the crowd is inconsistent with the heroism that is depicted in some of Nolan's films. Yet that is precisely Nolan's signature contribution to the blockbuster and superhero genres, that his protagonists can save the world and yet also leave unanswered many questions about their actions and the condition of that world. As Peters (2015: 419, 422) puts it, speaking specifically of Batman in *The Dark Knight*, Nolan '"makes strange" the traditional superhero mythos', his heroes only serving as a 'temporary measure to address a specific crisis' rather than effecting a permanent change in the system. Heroes are not heroes by virtue of transcending the human condition and the social circumstances that shape them. In Nolan's hermeneutic circle, this transcendence or escape is not possible, as even the heroes are shaped by social circumstances, and their actions in turn perpetuate social conditions. The historical war film *Dunkirk* offers Nolan the best opportunity to reinforce this point, depicting a 'miraculous' event which is no great military victory but merely the escape from annihilation, in which individuals (whose individuality for most of the film is blurred by their uniforms and the dirt and grease which covers them) scrabble and stumble towards survival, but where the outcome is nevertheless cheered by the nation.

Yet Nolan is no gloomy and cynical postmodernist, and does offer glimpses of hope, in the actions of some individuals which stand out against the grain of the crowd. But what is the audience to make of individuals like Cooper, Batman, Farrier and other lesser characters who display a selflessness and sacrifice at odds with the actions of the masses? Unable to change the social systems that are seen to shape and condition them, they often do not even succeed in getting others to emulate their example or understand the principles for which they stand. Tellingly, Nolan's most noble-seeming heroes do not succeed in giving their lives for their fellow men, although all attempt or appear to do so: Cooper is rescued from the shuttle, Batman ejects after putting the plane on autopilot, Farrier is captured and his fate uncertain, Neil is caught in a perpetual loop where he is simultaneously alive and dead. Those who do end up losing their lives in the course of seeking to benefit others – Foley and the Special Forces soldiers in *The Dark Knight Rises*, George and Gibson in *Dunkirk* – do so in confused melees, perhaps without anyone else being the wiser, and the beneficial effect of their lives is not at all clear. Nolan undercuts the very idea of heroic sacrifice by denying his characters either the clear moral purpose and result in sacrificing their lives, or else the actual deaths in the course of carrying out a noble intent.

The intent, in Nolan's moral schema, does matter. Nolan's films show a moral sensibility akin to that of the Utilitarian social thinkers, for whom the individual's choices and actions in society should result in 'greatest happiness of the whole community' that is possible

(Bentham 1952: 91). The zero-sum scenarios that Nolan depicts in many of his films mean that moral decisions are by no means easy, and sometimes it seems impossible for the protagonists to act without having negative or unintended consequences. Yet Nolan asks his audiences to consider that the intention to serve the 'greatest happiness of the whole community' might be the basis for the moral redemption of society, even when the results are qualified. No matter how fraught that intention is, how much it is problematized by imperfect knowledge and mixed motives, there is something admirable in the individual who believes in serving his fellow man and putting the interests of others before his own. It is the basis of the heroism of Batman, Commissioner Gordon, Cooper, Murphy, Farrier, George and others, the triumphalism that is undeniably present in Nolan's filmic treatment of their actions.

If indeed Nolan values the good intention whatever its complicated evidentiary bases and outcomes, he is not alone in validating it as the basis of moral action. For Immanuel Kant, 'the moral worth of an action does not depend on the result expected from it, and so too does not depend on any principle of action that needs to borrow its motive from this expected result' (Kant 1964: 69). Since results are unpredictable and contingent on circumstances, the only thing that can form the basis of an unconditional moral judgement is intention, or what Kant calls 'the good will':

A good will is not good because of what it effects or accomplishes – because of its fitness for attaining some proposed end: it is good through its willing alone – that is, good in itself.

(Kant 1964: 62)

This concept allows Kant to postulate that a moral act is one in which 'my maxim should become a universal law' (Kant 1964: 70), applicable to all men in all situations.

Kant would thus not allow Professor Brand's lie to trap the astronauts into fulfilling Plan B, since the maxim of 'using deceit to accomplish what I alone judge to be the best result' could not possibly be adopted as a universal law. Even less could the maxim behind Dormer's self-preserving lies, or Mann's selfish abandonment of the other astronauts, or the narrow tribalism of the (majority of the) civilian ferry passengers or the policeman who tries to kill Reese to protect his wife in the hospital, serve as the basis of a universal law. Any action which preserves the interests of the individual actor, or that of his narrow circle, fails Kant's notion of universal law because it could only result in particular laws (serving party A and group X) at conflict with other particular laws (serving party B and group Y). As we have seen, Nolan depicts the moral failings of a number of his protagonists whose actions, no matter how justified in their own minds, do not advance 'the social feelings of mankind; the desire to be in unity with our fellow creatures' (Mill 1910: 29).

If Nolan's heroes ultimately deserve something of the 'reverence' that for Kant (1964: 71) is the natural human response to a moral maxim, it is because their course of action evinces a 'good will' that intends to serve the broadest social category available to them, so that it can reasonably be extrapolated into a universal law. For all his flaws, Cooper desires to save as many people as possible – the whole of the existing population of Earth together with his own family, as well as the 5000 embryos. His own astronaut ambitions may be mixed into his actions, but expressed as a Kantian maxim, Cooper's decision to risk his own life to rescue not just his family but all of earth's remaining population, would make for an acceptable universal law. So would Batman's dedication to save Gotham's citizens, if expressed as the law that 'one should do good to one's fellow citizens to the extent of one's legitimate ability', thus avoiding any excuse of his extralegal measures. So would the efforts of Farrier, Gibson, George and others, if expressed as a universal law of 'good will' towards those in need of saving. So would the actions of the Protagonist and his circle, if expressed as the law of preserving the lives of those who live at present against those who aim at certain humanicide (even when that act of preservation is offset against the uncertain and unknowable interests of generations yet to come). There are no utopian societies or ideal social conditions in Nolan's films, and all characters (as proxies for the audience) struggle with unreliable knowledge and conflicted decisions. While Nolan does not gloss over his protagonists' moral failings, he does (especially in his later films) encourage the envisioning of a moral principle that can transcend the problems of society.

Not simply a gloomy postmodernist, Nolan lives in hope – and encourages his audiences to do the same. If he mirrors to audiences their own status as men in the crowd, trapped in the hermeneutic circle of inception and social contradiction, Nolan nevertheless challenges the viewer to take a 'leap of faith' by imagining and acting on something higher. It is up to each viewer, as it is for Nolan's protagonists, to decide for themselves if they wish to take that leap, and if so, to construct the moral bases on which it would be possible.

BIBLIOGRAPHY

Aronowitz, Stanley, 1988, 'Postmodernism and Politics', *The Politics of Postmodernism*, ed. Andrew Ross, Minneapolis: University of Minnesota Press, 46–62.

Barkman, Adam, 2012, 'Inception, Teaching, and Hypnosis: The Ethics of Idea-Giving', *Inception and Philosophy: Because It's Never Just a Dream*, ed. David Kyle Johnson and William Irwin, Hoboken, NJ: John Wiley and Sons, 140–51.

Baudrillard, Jean, 1994, *Simulacra and Simulation*, trans. Sheila Faria Glaser, Ann Arbor: University of Michigan Press.

Bauman, Zygmunt, 1997, *Postmodernity and Its Discontents*, Cambridge: Polity Press.

Bentham, Jeremy, 1952, 'The Philosophy of Economic Science', *Jeremy Bentham's Economic Writings*, ed. W. Stark, 3 vols, London: George Allen and Unwin, Volume I, 79–120.

Berman, Eliza, 2017, 'Christopher Nolan: *Dunkirk* Is My Most Experimental Film Since *Memento*', *Time* 19 July, online at: https://time.com/4864049/dunkirk-christopher-nolan-interview/ [accessed 17 June 2020].

Bernard, Catherine, 2017, 'Christopher Nolan's Inception: Spectacular Speculations', *Screen* 58: 2, 229–36.

Bewes, Timothy, 1997, *Cynicism and Postmodernity*, London: Verso.

Bott, Nicholas, 2013, 'How Can Satan Cast out Satan? Violence and the Birth of the Sacred in Christopher Nolan's *The Dark Knight*', *Contagion: Journal of Violence, Mimesis, and Culture*, 20, 239–51.

Botting, Fred, 1996, *Gothic*, London: Routledge.

Botz-Bornstein, Thorsten, 2011, 'Who's Putting Ideas in Your Head?', *Inception and Philosophy: Ideas to Die For*, ed. Thorsten Botz-Bornstein, Chicago: Open Court, vii–ix.

Bright, William, 2004, *Native American Place Names of the United States*, Norman: University of Oklahoma Press.

Brislin, Tom, 2016. 'Time, Ethics, and the Films of Christopher Nolan', *Visual Communication Quarterly* 23: 4, 199–209.

Capps, Robert, 2010, 'Q & A: Christopher Nolan on Dreams, Architecture and Ambiguity', *Wired* 29 November, online at: https://www.wired.com/2010/11/pl-inception-nolan/ [accessed 30 June 2020].

Caughie, John, 1981, 'Introduction', *Theories of Authorship*, ed. John Caughie, London: Routledge, 9–16.

Crowe, Cameron (directed and written), 1996, *Jerry Maguire*, U.S.A.: TriStar Pictures, Gracie Films, Vinyl Films.

Derrida, Jacques, 1974, *Of Grammatology*, trans. Gayatri Chakravorty Spivak, Baltimore: Johns Hopkins University Press.

Dreyer, Randolph, 2009. 'Clap If You Believe in Batman', *Perspectives in Psychiatric Care* 45: 1, 80–1.

Eberl, Jason T. and George A. Dunn (ed.), 2017, *The Philosophy of Christopher Nolan*, Lanham: Lexington Books.

Faithful, George, 2014, 'Salvation from Illusion, Salvation by Illusion: The Gospel According to Christopher Nolan', *Implicit Religion* 14: 4, 405–16.

Fischer, Mark, 2011, 'The Lost Unconscious: Delusions and Dreams in Inception', *Film Quarterly* 64: 3, 37–45.

Fitzpatrick, John R. and David Kyle Johnson, 2012, 'Inception and Free Will: Are They Compatible?', *Inception and Philosophy: Because It's Never Just a Dream*, ed. David Johnson, Hoboken: John Wiley and Sons, 152–66.

Flisfeder, Matthew, 2017, *Postmodern Theory and Blade Runner*, London: Bloomsbury.

Fluck, Winfried, 2001, 'Crime, Guilt and Subjectivity in "Film Noir,"' *Amerikastudien/American Studies* 46: 3, 379–408.

Foucault, Michel, 1977, 'What Is an Author', *Michel Foucault: Language, Counter-Memory, Practice*, ed. Donald F. Bouchard, Ithaca: Cornell University Press, 113–38.

Freud, Sigmund, 1984a, 'The Unconscious', in *On Metapsychology: The Theory of Psychoanalysis* (Penguin Freud Library vol. 11), trans. James Strachey, London: Penguin Books, 159–222.

Freud, Sigmund, 1984b, 'Beyond the Pleasure Principle', in *On Metapsychology: The Theory of Psychoanalysis* (Penguin Freud Library vol. 11), trans. James Strachey, London: Penguin Books, 269–338.

Freud, Sigmund, 2005, *Civilization and Its Discontents*, trans. James Strachey, New York: W. W. Norton.

Furness, Hannah, 2017, 'New Dunkirk Film Won't Feature Churchill So It Doesn't Get "Bogged Down" with Politics', *The Telegraph* 7 July, online at: https://www.telegraph.co.uk/news/2017/07/07/new-dunkirk-film-wont-feature-churchill-doesnt-get-bogged-politics/#:~:text=But%20a%20new%20blockbuster%20film,%E2%80%9Cbogged%20down%E2%80%9D%20in%20politics [accessed 7 December 2020].

Garcia, J. L. A, 2006, 'White Nights of the Soul: Christopher Nolan's *Insomnia* and the Renewal of Moral Reflection in Film', *Logos: A Journal of Catholic Thought and Culture*, 9: 4, 82–117.

Gervais, Marc, 1999, *Ingmar Bergman: Magician and Prophet*, Montreal and Kingston: McGill-Queen's University Press.

Goh, Robbie B. H., 2008, 'Myths of Reversal: Backwards Narratives, Normative Schizophrenia and the Culture of Causal Agnosticism', *Social Semiotics* 18: 1, 61–77.

Grant, Adam, 2017, 'Christopher Nolan Wants You to Silence Your Phones', *Esquire* 19 July, online at: https://www.esquire.com/entertainment/movies/a55985/christopher-nolan-interview/ [accessed 2 July 2020].

Hobbes, Thomas, 1968, *Leviathan*, ed. C. B. Macpherson, Harmondsworth: Penguin.

Hunt, Ailsa, 2019, 'Servian Readings of Religion in the *Georgics*', *Reflections and New Perspectives on Virgil's Georgics*, ed. Bobby Xinyue and Nicholas Freer, London: Bloomsbury Academic, pp. 139–53.

Hutcheon, Linda, 1989, *The Politics of Postmodernism*, London: Routledge.

Hynes, Eric, 2018, 'Cannes Interview: Christopher Nolan', *Film Comment* 17 May, online at: https://www.filmcomment.com/blog/interview-christopher-nolan/ [accessed 2 July 2020].

Ittmann, Karl, 1995, *Work, Gender and Family in Victorian England*, Houndmills: MacMillan.

Jalland, Pat, 1996, *Death in the Victorian Family*, Oxford: Oxford University Press.

Jameson, Fredric, 2003, *Postmodernism: Or, The Cultural Logic of Late Capitalism*, Durham: Duke University Press.

Johnson, Vilja, 2014, '"It's What You Do That Defines You": Christopher Nolan's Batman as Moral Philosopher', *Journal of Popular Culture*, 47: 5, 952–66.

Kant, Immanuel, 1964, *Groundwork of the Metaphysic of Morals*, trans. H. J. Paton, New York: Harper Perennial.

Kayhan, Sezen, 2014, *Fragments of Tragedy in Postmodern Film*, Newcastle Upon Tyne: Cambridge Scholars.

Kiang, Jessica, 2020, '"Tenet" Review: Christopher Nolan's Time-Bending Take on James Bond', *New York Times* 21 August, online at: https://www.nytimes.com/2020/08/21/movies/tenet-review-christopher-nolan.html [accessed 19 March 2021].

Klein, Andy, 2001, 'Everything You Wanted to Know about *Memento*', *Salon* 28 June, online at: https://www.salon.com/2001/06/28/memento_analysis/ [accessed 18 July 2020].

Klotz, Marcia, 2019, 'Of Time Loops and Derivatives: Christopher Nolan's *Interstellar* and the Logic of the Futures Market', *CR: The New Centennial Review*, 19: 1, 277–97.

Lackey, Douglas, 2019, 'The Auteur Theory in the Age of the Mini-Series', *The Palgrave Handbook of the Philosophy of Film and Motion Pictures*, ed. Noel Carroll, Laura T. Di Summa and Shawn Loht, Cham, Switzerland: Palgrave MacMillan, 543–50.

Lane, Anthony, 2002, 'Odd Couples: *Insomnia* and *Late Marriage*', *The New Yorker* 20 May, online at: https://www.newyorker.com/magazine/2002/05/27/odd-couples-2 [accessed 1 August 2020].

Lang, Brent, 2017, 'Christopher Nolan Gets Candid on the State of Movies, Rise of TV, and Spielberg's Influence', *Variety*, 7 November, online at: https://variety.com/2017/film/news/christopher-nolan-dunkirk-oscars-movies-tv-spielberg-1202607836/ [accessed 2 July 2020].

Lewis-Krause, Gideon, 2014, 'The Exacting, Expansive Mind of Christopher Nolan', *The New York Times Magazine*, 30 October, online at: https://www.nytimes.com/2014/11/02/magazine/the-exacting-expansive-mind-of-christopher-nolan.html [accessed 15 June 2020].

Lockhart, Aidan A., 2018, 'Capes, Cowls, and the Fragments of Ideology: Toward a Framework for Revealing Retributive Ideology in Film', *Journal of Popular Culture*, 51: 1, 215–35.

Luhr, William, 2012, *Film Noir*, Chichester: Wiley-Blackwell.

Lyotard, Jean Francois, 1989, 'Discussions, or Phrasing "After Auschwitz,"' *The Lyotard Reader*, ed. Andrew Benjamin, Oxford: Blackwell, 360–92.

Malloy, Daniel P., 2012, 'How to Hijack a Mind: *Inception* and the Ethics of Heist Films', *Inception and Philosophy: Because It's Never Just a Dream*, ed. David Kyle Johnson and William Irwin, Hoboken, NJ: John Wiley and Sons, 125–39.

Malthus, T. R., 1993, *An Essay on the Principle of Population*, Oxford: Oxford University Press.

May, Todd, 1995, *The Moral Theory of Poststructuralism*, University Park, PA: University of Pennsylvania Press.

McEwan, Ian, 2006, *Enduring Love*, London: Vintage Books.

McHale, Brian, 2015, *The Cambridge Introduction to Postmodernism*, New York: Cambridge University Press.

Mill, J. S., 1910, *Utilitarianism, Liberty, Representative Government*, introduction by A. D. Lindsay, London: J. M Dent and Sons, 1910.

Muller, John P. and William J. Richardson (eds), 1988, *The Purloined Poe: Lacan, Derrida, and Psychoanalytic Reading*, Baltimore: Johns Hopkins University Press.

Myers, Scott, 2017, 'Interview (Written): Christopher Nolan', *Go into The Story*, 22 July, online at: https://gointothestory.blcklst.com/interview-written-christopher-nolan-f4fe29bc969f [accessed 28 June 2020].

Nestingen, Andrew, 2013, *The Cinema of Aki Kaurismäki: Contrarian Stories*, London: Wallflower Press.

Newbould, Chris, 2018, 'Has Michael Caine Ended the "Inception" Ending Debate?', *The National* 21 August, online at: https://www.thenational.ae/arts-culture/film/has-michael-caine-ended-the-inception-ending-debate-1.762335 [accessed 17 August 2020].

Newby, Richard, 2020, "'Tenet" and the Past and Future of Christopher Nolan', *The Hollywood Reporter* 23 December, online at: https://www.hollywoodreporter.com/heat-vision/tenet-and-the-past-and-future-of-christopher-nolan [accessed 19 March 2021].

Nietzsche, Friedrich, 1961, *Thus Spoke Zarathurstra*, trans. R. J. Hollingdale, Harmondsworth: Penguin.

Nietzsche, Friedrich, 1968, *Twilight of the Idols and The Anti-Christ*, trans. R. J. Hollingdale, Harmondsworth: Penguin.

Nietzsche, Friedrich, 2002, *Beyond Good and Evil: Prelude to a Philosophy of the Future*, trans. Judith Norman, Cambridge: Cambridge University Press.

Nolan, Christopher (directed and written), 1998, *Following*, United Kingdom: Next Wave Films.

Nolan, Christopher (directed and written), 2000, *Memento*, USA: Newmarket Capital Group, Summit Entertainment, Team Todd, I Remember Productions.

Nolan, Christopher (directed), 2002, *Insomnia*, USA: Alcon Entertainment, Witt/Thomas Productions, Section Eight, Insomnia Productions, Summit Entertainment.

Nolan, Christopher (directed and screenplay), 2005, *Batman Begins*, USA: Warner Brothers, Syncopy, DC Comics, Legendary Entertainment, Patalex III Productions.

Nolan, Christopher (directed and screenplay), 2006, *The Prestige*, USA: Touchstone Pictures, Warner Brothers, Newmarket Productions, Syncopy.

Nolan, Christopher (directed and screenplay), 2008, *The Dark Knight*, USA: Warner Brothers, Legendary Entertainment, Syncopy, DC Comics.

Nolan, Christopher (directed and written), 2010, *Inception*, USA: Warner Brothers, Legendary Entertainment, Syncopy.

Nolan, Christopher (directed and screenplay), 2012, *The Dark Knight Rises*, USA: Warner Brothers, Legendary Entertainment, DC Entertainment, Syncopy, DC Comics.

Nolan, Christopher (directed and written), 2014, *Interstellar*, USA: Paramount Pictures, Warner Brothers, Legendary Entertainment, Syncopy, Lynda Obst Productions.

Nolan, Christopher (directed and written), 2017, *Dunkirk*, USA: Syncopy, Warner Brothers, Dombey Street Productions, Kaap Holland Film.

Nolan, Christopher (directed and written), 2020, *Tenet*, USA: Warner Brothers, Syncopy.

Peters, Timothy D., 2015, 'Beyond the Limits of the Law: A Christological Reading of Christopher Nolan's *The Dark Knight*', *Griffith Law Review* 24: 3, 418–45.

Poe, Edgar Allan, 1993, 'The Purloined Letter', *Tales of Mystery and Imagination*, ed. John S. Whitley, Hertfordshire: Wordsworth Editions, 132–47.

Resner, Jeffrey, 2012, 'The Traditionalist', *DGA Quarterly* Spring, online at: https://www.dga.org/Craft/DGAQ/All-Articles/1202-Spring-2012/DGA-Interview-Christopher-Nolan.aspx [accessed 17 June 2020].

Russell, Bertrand, 1945, *A History of Western Philosophy*, New York: Simon and Schuster.

Russell, Patrick Kent, 2017, 'Christopher Nolan's *The Dark Knight* Trilogy as a Noir View of American Social Tensions', *Interdisciplinary Humanities* 33: 1, 171–86.

Schimmelpfennig, Annette, 2017, 'Capitalism and Schizophrenia in Gotham City: The Fragile Masculinities of Christopher Nolan's The Dark Knight Trilogy', *Gender Forum* 62, 3–20.

Simmel, Georg, 1978, *The Philosophy of Money*, trans. David Frisby, London: Routledge.

Smith, Adam, 1759, *The Theory of Moral Sentiments*, London: A. Millar.

Smith, Adam, 1937, *An Inquiry into the Nature and Causes of the Wealth of Nations*, New York: Modern Library.

Stephan, Matthias, 2019, *Defining Literary Postmodernism for the Twenty-First Century*, Cham, Switzerland: Palgrave MacMillan.

Tallman, Ruth, 2012, 'Was It All a Dream? Why Nolan's Answer Doesn't Matter', *Inception and Philosophy: Because It's Never Just a Dream*, ed. David Kyle Johnson and William Irwin, Hoboken, NJ: John Wiley and Sons, 17–30.

Terjesen, Andrew, 2012, 'Even If It Is a Dream, We Should Still Care', *Inception and Philosophy: Because It's Never Just a Dream*, ed. David Kyle Johnson and William Irwin, Hoboken, NJ: John Wiley and Sons, 46–61.

Testerman, Janet, 2011, 'You Have No Idea', *Inception and Philosophy: Ideas to Die For*, ed. Thorsten Botz-Bornstein, Chicago: Open Court, 67–80.

Toth, Margaret A., 2015, '*Memento*'s Postmodern *Noir* Fantasy: Place, Domesticity, and Gender Identity', *The Cinema of Christopher Nolan: Imagining the Impossible*, ed. Jacqueline Furby and Stuart Joy, London: Wallflower Press, 74–84.

Tseng, Tsiaoi and John A. Bateman, 2011, 'Multimodal Narrative Construction in Christopher Nolan's *Memento*: A Description of Analytic Method', *Visual Communication* 11: 1, 91–119.

Watson, Paul, 1996, 'Critical Approaches to Hollywood Cinema: Authorship, Genre and Stars', *An Introduction to Film Studies*, ed. Jill Nelmes, London: Routledge, 130–83.

Webber, Andrew J., 1996, *The Doppelgänger: Double Visions in German Literature*, Oxford: Clarendon Press.

Weijers, Dan, 2012, 'Reality Doesn't Really Matter', *Inception and Philosophy: Because It's Never Just a Dream*, ed. David Kyle Johnson and William Irwin, Hoboken, NJ: John Wiley and Sons, 92–107.

Welk, Brian, 2020, 'Christopher Nolan Says He Crashed a Real 747 in "Tenet" Because It Was Cheaper than Using CG', *The Wrap* 27 May, online at: https://www.thewrap.com/christopher-nolan-tenet-747-plane-stunt-interview/ [accessed 2 July 2020].

Wenmackers, Sylvia, 2011, 'How to Keep Track of Reality', *Inception and Philosophy: Ideas to Die For*, ed. Thorsten Botz-Bornstein, Chicago: Open Court, 3–24.

Wilberding, James, 2012, 'Curbing One's Appetites in Plato's Republic', *Plato and the Divided Self*, ed. Rachel Barney, Ted Brennan and Charles Brittain, Cambridge: Cambridge University Press, 128–49.

Winchur, Drew, 2012, 'Ideology in Christopher Nolan's *Inception*', *Cineaction* 88, 44–7.

Winstead, Nick, 2015, '"As a Symbol I Can Be Incorruptible": How Christopher Nolan De-Queered the Batman of Joel Schumacher', *Journal of Popular Culture* 48: 3, 572–85.

Zehfuss, Maja, 2002, *Constructivism in International Relations: The Politics of Reality*, Cambridge: Cambridge University Press.

INDEX